IN-SERVICE EDUCATION WITHIN
THE SCHOOL

Unwin Education Books

Education Since 1800 IVOR MORRISH
Physical Education for Teaching BARBARA CHURCHER
Organising and Integrating the Infant Day JOY TAYLOR
The Philosophy of Education: An Introduction HARRY SCHOFIELD
Assessment and Testing: An Introduction HARRY SCHOFIELD
Education: Its Nature and Purpose M. V. C. JEFFREYS
Learning in the Primary School KENNETH HASLAM
The Sociology of Education: An Introduction IVOR MORRISH
Developing a Curriculum AUDREY and HOWARD NICHOLLS
Teacher Education and Cultural Change H. DUDLEY PLUNKETT and
  JAMES LYNCH
Reading and Writing in the First School JOY TAYLOR
Approaches to Drama DAVID A. MALE
Aspects of Learning BRIAN O'CONNELL
Focus on Meaning JOAN TOUGH
Moral Education WILLIAM KAY
Concepts in Primary Education JOHN E. SADLER
Moral Philosophy for Education ROBIN BARROW
Principles of Classroom Learning and Perception RICHARD J. MUELLER
Education and the Community ERIC MIDWINTER
Creative Teaching AUDREY and HOWARD NICHOLLS
The Preachers of Culture MARGARET MATHIESON
Mental Handicap: An Introduction DAVID EDEN
Aspects of Educational Change IVOR MORRISH
Beyond Initial Reading JOHN POTTS
The Foundations of Maths in the Infant School JOY TAYLOR
Common Sense and the Curriculum ROBIN BARROW
The Second 'R' WILLIAM HARPIN
The Diploma Disease RONALD DORE
The Development of Meaning JOAN TOUGH
The Place of Commonsense in Educational Thought LIONEL ELVIN
Language in Teaching and Learning HAZEL FRANCIS
Patterns of Education in the British Isles NIGEL GRANT and ROBERT BELL
Philosophical Foundations for the Curriculum ALLEN BRENT
World Faiths in Education W. OWEN COLE
Classroom Language: What Sort? JILL RICHARDS
Philosophy and Human Movement DAVID BEST
Secondary Schools and the Welfare Network DAPHNE JOHNSON *et al.*
Educating Adolescent Girls E. M. CHANDLER
Classroom Observation of Primary School Children RICHARD W. MILLS
Essays on Educators R. S. PETERS
Comparative Education: Some Considerations of Method BRIAN HOLMES
Education and the Individual BRENDA COHEN
Moral Development and Moral Education R. S. PETERS
In-Service Education within the School ROLAND W. MORANT

In-Service Education within the School

ROLAND W. MORANT
Head of Division of In-Service and School-Based Studies,
Crewe and Alsager College of Higher Education

London
GEORGE ALLEN & UNWIN
Boston   Sydney

George Allen & Unwin (Publishers) Ltd,
40 Museum Street, London WC1A 1LU, UK

George Allen & Unwin (Publishers) Ltd,
Park Lane, Hemel Hempstead, Herts HP2 4TE, UK

Allen & Unwin Inc.,
9 Winchester Terrace, Winchester, Mass 01890, USA

George Allen & Unwin Australia Pty Ltd,
8 Napier Street, North Sydney, NSW 2060, Australia

First published in 1981

British Library Cataloguing in Publication Data

Morant, Roland W.
  In-service education within the school. – (Unwin education books)
1. Teachers – In-service training
I. Title
371.1'46   LB1731
ISBN 0-04-370111-6
ISBN 0-04-370112-4 pbk

Library of Congress Cataloging in Publication Data

Morant, Roland William.
  In-service education within the school.
(Unwin education books)
Bibliography: p.
Includes index.
1. Teachers – In-service training. I. Title. II. Series.
LB1731.M63   371.1'46   81-12668
ISBN 0-04-370111-6   AACR2
ISBN 0-04-370112-4 (pbk.)

Set in 10 on 11 point Times by Computape (Pickering) Ltd,
and printed in Great Britain
by Billing and Sons, Guildford, London and Worcester

Contents

Preface   *Page*   ix

Acknowledgement   xi

1 The Meaning of In-Service Education   1
   Education and training
   Teachers' professional needs

2 In-Service Work outside the School   14
   The providing bodies
   In-service activities
   Course validation
   Funding of in-service work

3 The School and In-Service Education   25
   An evolving in-service picture
   The school as a base for in-service work

4 The School-Focused Approach   40
   Some allied concepts and their distinction
   Some examples of school-focused work

5 The School-Directed Programme: an Action Model   51
   Planned change in school
   Bringing about planned change
   In-service education in support of planned change
   Educational research and the school

6 Developing and Implementing the Programme   67
   The school's in-service policies and structures
   Procedures and strategies
   In-service priorities

7 Evaluating the Programme   80
   Evaluation today
   Who should undertake evaluation?
   What should be evaluated and why?
   How should evaluation be conducted?

8 Resourcing the Programme   95
   Potential resources
   Consultancy and the school
   Programme constraints

Directory of Resources   106
Information that will be of help to teachers developing
in-service programmes in their own schools: (*A*) journals,
(*B*) books, (*C*) pamphlets and booklets, (*D*) some
national bodies

Index   123

Preface

This short guide is intended to give practical help to all teachers, primary and secondary, who wish to plan, carry out and evaluate a programme of in-service education within their school, a programme which – according to particular circumstances – may be envisaged for the whole staff, for a department or for a small group of teachers with a special interest or responsibility.

For many years it was widely accepted that the initial training given to teachers – whether by certificate or degree route – equipped them for a lifetime's career in the education service. Such in-service training as there was, almost invariably offered by agencies and institutions at a distance from the school and mounted off the school premises, tended to be supplementary in character to initial forms of training. Moreover, it had two main purposes, one of which was to provide short courses of the 'tips for teachers' type and the other to provide long courses usually leading to diplomas of marketable value that would enhance promotion prospects.

Until very recently, the notion of in-service education in school was one that was barely perceived. To be expected or encouraged to undertake training specifically related to the teacher's own classroom or school was something that simply did not happen, except possibly to someone in the probationary year. Only now can it safely be said that teachers' on-the-job education is able to offer those experiences which have particular relevance to the problems and requirements of individual schools. In addition, further or 'post-experience' professional education of teachers, devised and executed by themselves within the context of their own school, can be a powerful instrument for underpinning desirable innovation and renewal, and for increasing personal motivation.

In order to meet this broad aim, the guide examines the general meaning of in-service education in relation to teachers' professional and academic needs. It summarises the provision of in-service education which traditionally has been made available outside the school, and suggests how the idea of in-service education focused on the individual school could be of especial help to its teachers. The guide shows how this latter kind of work can be planned and implemented; and finally it discusses possible resources, internal and external to the school, on which teachers may wish to draw for the work, giving actual details of such resources in a directory.

Acknowledgement

The author acknowledges with gratitude permission granted by Messrs Eye To Eye Publications Ltd to reproduce an article, 'Consultancy work in schools', which appears substantially unchanged in the section 'Consultancy and the School' in Chapter 8 (see note 4 at the end of the chapter).

IN-SERVICE EDUCATION WITHIN THE SCHOOL

Chapter 1

The Meaning of In-Service Education

Within the teaching profession and beyond it, few topics evoke such a ready response as in-service education. Nearly everyone – whether teacher, adviser or educational administrator – seems convinced of its value. But before we join in the chorus of approval, we should be clear as to what the term means. This opening chapter offers a general description of in-service education, within which framework in-service work specifically involving the teacher's own school can properly be understood. The related concepts of in-service education and training are examined; and finally the chapter turns to looking at professional needs which may be taken as a starting-point for planning teachers' continuing education.

EDUCATION AND TRAINING

It is probably easier to say *when* in-service education should occur than to give an immediate definition. It is the education intended to support and assist the professional development that teachers ought to experience throughout their working lives. Its starting-point thus should be marked by the occasion when the newly qualified entrant to the teaching profession takes up his first appointment in school. Its finishing-point coincides with retirement. That suggests that in-service education in one form or another could be experienced by a teacher, if he were so disposed, for a span of perhaps forty years.

What does in-service actually consist of? Some share the opinion that in-service education should be cast widely to include virtually any experience to which a teacher, voluntarily or involuntarily, may be exposed (the view that 'All experience is good experience'). Professional development, according to this line of thought, will be strengthened by almost all activities undertaken by him after he has started to teach. But there is an obvious danger in believing that almost any experience or activity will be linked directly to the teacher's work in classroom or school. Professional development should be served by something more relevant than educational spin-off that may result from general adult education.

The other prevailing view is that in-service education should be closely and specifically aligned to the teacher's professional working life. Some years ago in a book on teachers' in-service views and preferences, Brian Cane[1] included a definition of in-service training which ran as follows:

> In-service training is taken to include all those courses and activities in which a serving teacher may participate for the purpose of extending his professional knowledge, interest or skill. Preparation for a degree, diploma or other qualification subsequent to initial training is included within this definition.

It will be noted that the key to this tighter and more central approach is the purposive nature of the intended experiences. Such studies should be planned deliberately to bring about certain changes that will lead to a subsequent improvement in the teacher's performance in school.

Purposive in-service education may have a variety of guises. As the James Committee[2] in 1972 suggested, it can cover a wide spectrum ranging from evening meetings and discussions to weekend conferences and other short-term activities. Though often highly motivating to the teacher, these experiences – frequently characterised by their irregularity and casual nature – do not necessarily lead to tangible results in terms of classroom performance. Neither do they automatically improve his promotion chances.

At the other end of the spectrum are the substantial in-service activities – substantial that is in their length and/or intellectual demand. Often they may be sustained and carefully structured courses leading to award-bearing qualifications which undoubtedly do bring incremental benefit or promotion. Although not everyone agrees on what constitutes the essence of in-service education, nevertheless, as the James Committee maintained, it clearly comprehends the whole range of relevant activities whereby teachers can extend their personal education, develop their professional competence and improve their understanding of educational principles.

It will be noted that Cane wrote about teachers' in-service training rather than their education. Indeed there are some educationalists today who would prefer to stress the concept of training in preference to that of education. On the grounds that the goals of education are diffuse and long-term and thus inappropriate, Henderson[3] uses the term 'in-service training', defining the latter as 'structured activities designed exclusively or primarily to improve professional performance'. He justifies his choice on the basis that training implies a more direct link between learning and action and is therefore easier to measure, the results of training being more readily usable in bringing about practical improvement.

There may be some sympathy for this view. But it is undeniable that there are many in-service study experiences belonging to the short term (for instance, involving consultation or group discussion) which, though not easily assessed or readily fitting the training mould, are clearly of considerable benefit to the participants. One must ask who would deny teachers such opportunities for in-service study when training as such was not necessarily taking place.

There is little doubt that there is a distinction between education and training, and the difference is not unimportant. Training is concerned with the acquisition of skills and techniques using standardised learning procedures and sequences. One instance might be learning the mechanics of constructing a school timetable; another, finding out how to mark a class register and total it up at the end of the term.

In contrast, the broader concept of in-service education is bound up with the notion of bringing about teachers' professional, academic and personal development through the provision of a whole series of study experiences and activities of which training should be rated as but one aspect. Hence in-service training should not be considered as an alternative to in-service education but as a part of the total framework of in-service education.

That a close connection exists between the two is recognised, as is illustrated in official documents and other publications where increasingly the acronym 'INSET'[4] (standing for 'in-service education and training') is used. Arguably, this acronym indicates a false parallel and possibly equal relationship between education and training. For this reason it is probably safer to employ the phrase 'in-service education' (which by implication is inclusive of its training aspect) as the comprehensive term; and in this sense we shall henceforth employ it.

Having cleared some of the ground, it is now possible to suggest a general statement indicating the purpose of in-service education. This is that in-service education aims to widen and deepen teachers' knowledge, understanding and expertise (including skills, techniques and powers of judgement) in respect of their professional work, by means of activities designed primarily to attain this purpose.

If this is acceptable as an all-sufficient statement, it needs to be elaborated in terms of some more specific objectives. Probably one of the best sets of objectives is provided by the Advisory Committee on the Supply and Training of Teachers,[5] namely, to enable teachers

(a) to evaluate their own work and attitudes in conjunction with their professional colleagues in other parts of the education service;
(b) to develop their professional competence, confidence and relevant knowledge;
(c) to develop criteria which would help them to assess their own teaching roles in relation to a changing society for which the schools must equip their pupils; and
(d) to advance their careers.

The chief thing to be noticed about these four objectives is their catholicity in that they are intended collectively to assist teachers to relate their in-service studies to their schools, the wider educational scene and society in general. At the same time, the all-inclusiveness of these objectives permits and encourages teachers' career aspirations (including those relating to promotion) to be met.

Thus in-service education starts by helping teachers to examine their existing practices in school in a critical manner (Objective (a)), possibly with the help of other people working in the school or outside it. This will enable them to identify their immediate professional problems and needs. As a result of this preliminary work, they should then be in a position to take action in meeting these needs (Objective (b)). Following on, this should lead to an identification of further professional needs springing from new perceptions concerning the relationship of their school and changing society (Objective (c)). Running parallel with this process of need identification and need realisation intended to help the school and its pupils, is the separate process of need identification and realisation leading to individual teachers' career renewal and advancement (Objective (d)).

TEACHERS' PROFESSIONAL NEEDS

If a starting-point for in-service education is teachers' professional needs, what is meant by such needs?

The individual teacher in his working life at school will inevitably experience problems – not necessarily serious or negative ones – that stem directly or indirectly from professional contact and involvement with pupils and colleagues. For example, an inexperienced teacher might become aware through comments made by his head of department that his methods of displaying pupils' written work on the walls of his classroom are not up to the standard generally observed by other teachers in the department. Accordingly, the teacher finds himself in a condition of need.

One solution to this particular problem might be for the teacher to have an informal talk with one or other colleague having requisite knowledge of display techniques; another might be to attend an appropriate short course at the local teachers' centre. In either event his problem can be resolved and his professional need met or reduced. Responses like these, rendered informally by means of a conversation or formally through attendance at a course of study, may be interpreted as in-service education since they can be approximated with the general purpose of in-service education as previously defined.

The range and variety of professional needs will be predictably very wide and numerous. Many are likely to be met with by the practitioner in his classroom where he has specific and well-defined responsibilities for teaching a particular class or subject. His needs derive from his age, his personal and professional education, the sum of his teaching experience and his personality and temperament. Some of these needs may be relatively minor like requiring to know how to teach a rule of number, or more weighty like desiring to update one's subject knowledge at sixth-form teaching level.

The individual teacher will become aware of further needs within the context of a functional group of which he forms part in school: a department, a teaching team or even the senior management team of a secondary school. Such needs will be personal to him, but they will not be unique in time or place; other teachers in the same functional group will be experiencing similar if not precisely identical needs. Thus there might be a group of probationary teachers all possessing secret fears over keeping discipline at the start of their careers, or a group of otherwise experienced teachers wanting to learn how to introduce resource-based learning in their common teaching subject.

Moreover, a third distinct set of needs will be experienced by the individual teacher within the framework of the whole staff of the school. Thus all the teachers of a primary school might wish to make a study of the recent HMI survey on the primary curriculum.[6] Or the staff of a secondary school might wish to evaluate its pupil assessment procedures. Again, though the teachers may each meet with needs in their own way, many of these needs will seem to have a collective identity and will appear to be replicated to some degree among some or all members of the staff.

Responsibility for identifying needs, though the latter be expressed at different levels of organisation in the school, as far as possible should rest with individual teachers experiencing them and not be passed to colleagues however knowledgeable or understanding. A measure of true professionalism is the degree of autonomy that serving members of any calling actually have. Ideally, teachers should retain responsibility for their own in-service education and through this, for their personal career development. Arguably, until all professional needs can be met by the teacher taking action himself, it may not be possible for him to attain his full professional potential.

If we examine the substance of teachers' needs, we find that these needs correspond to four main types (Table 1.1).

(1) *Teachers' Induction Needs*

At least once and probably several times during his career, a teacher will embark on new and unfamiliar duties relating to a position to which he has just been appointed. The first occasion when this may happen is the time when the new entrant, having recently left college or university, starts work in school where he is required to complete a period of probation normally lasting a year. The process designed to smooth the probationer's path has been described as 'a systematic programme of professional initiation, guided experience and further study'[7] and is usually referred to as induction. Quite clearly, getting properly started in one's initial post as a qualified teacher is very important since the inexperienced novice can be made or broken in his beginning year. It is for this reason that recently considerable thought and effort at national and local levels has gone into devising induction programmes which enable smooth adjustment to be made. Proportionately more has been written about the probationary period of teaching than any other branch of in-service education, and this is reflected in the bibliographies appearing in the Directory of Resources at the end of the book.

But there are many other times when the teacher starts work in a new and untried sphere, and often the change may involve moving from one school to another. Promotion to head of department, deputy head or headteacher is an obvious example; a sideways move from one job to a similar one elsewhere is another.

The teacher is therefore likely to be faced with problems arising from, at best, a measure of inexperience or lack of confidence or, at worst, sheer ignorance of what the task entails. But irrespective of the demands of the new post, the teacher will experience induction needs which, more often than not, require to be dealt with from the day on which he is appointed and certainly not from when he actually commences work.

Table 1.1 *Career Situations and Teachers' Accompanying Professional Needs*

1	Period of probation at start of career	
2	Adjustment period immediately following appointment to a new post	INDUCTION NEEDS
3	Early career period; serving as subject or class teacher	
4	Middle career period; serving as head of department, etc.	EXTENSION NEEDS
5	Later career period; serving as deputy head or head	
6	Period towards end of gap in career	
7	Period prior to having to teach a subject or age-range not taught for a long time (e.g. since teaching practice)	REFRESHMENT NEEDS
8	Period of excessively repetitive professional experience (e.g. same post, same school, similar type of children)	
9	Period prior to internal redeployment	
10	Period prior to external redeployment	
11	Period of anticipated promotion	CONVERSION NEEDS
12	Period of ante-retirement	

When induction, as in the normal promotion situation, is not linked to a formal period of probation, the adjustment period tends to be brief, lasting perhaps no longer than a few weeks, 'to learn the job'. It follows logically that in-service activities designed to meet such induction needs will also have to be concentrated into an equivalent period of time. Intentionally, these activities will be professional in character rather than academic and therefore firmly practical in their aim. Because inevitably there will be guidance by one experienced practitioner of another, less experienced, practitioner during this adjustment period, much of this form of in-service education will depend on frequent and informal advice given in respect of a specific job or task which may be reinforced by short intensive formally organised courses in or out of school.

(2) *Teachers' Extension Needs*

Consider a teacher who has occupied a position in school for several years. By this time he ought to have overcome most of the difficulties encountered early on. Furthermore, he should have gained some solid experience and be capable of employing appropriate skills and techniques while performing his present duties. He should thus have reached a point in this stage of his career where he can achieve useful results in his teaching, marked by some economy of effort – a sign of increasing personal professionalism. He will now be ready to widen his professional and academic horizons by relating his existing responsibilities and duties, and acquired experiences, to the wider interests of the school and education service. Moreover, he may well be prompted to look for promotion.

In this situation, the individual teacher's needs will be varied and substantial. If his career happens to be in an early stage of development – for instance, he might be second in a fairly small department of a comprehensive school, on a Scale 2 post – he might wish to strengthen his subject teaching by reinforcing his academic knowledge and strengthening his subject methodology. If he is in the middle of his career, for example as head of department or head of year, he might want to obtain a better grasp of curriculum theory or obtain expertise in the principles of school management. If he holds a senior position, for example as deputy head or headteacher where subject teaching may not be his chief concern, his needs might be associated with school management, evaluation and assessment of performance, or knowledge of administration of the local education authority.

To meet such professional needs which can broadly be described as extension needs, in-service activities which have certain characteristics should be made available to teachers. These are that the work is likely to:

(a) be followed to an advanced level of attainment (and related to the fact that the teaching profession is moving fairly fast towards all-graduate status, with all new teachers now possessing first degrees);

(b) consist of in-depth study pursued normally over a relatively long period of time (say one year full-time, or two to three years part-time); and (*c*) almost all be award-bearing, at diploma or second degree level.

(3) *Teachers' Refreshment Needs*

According to the dictionary, to refresh means to reinvigorate, to reanimate and to restore. Each of these verbs suggests the nature of various professional needs which the majority of teachers experience from time to time in their careers.

First, those teachers may be identified who, after a period away from school, wish to be updated on teaching a particular age-range or subject studied some years earlier at college or university. The break in service might be due to several reasons of which the most common is likely to be that of married women leaving the profession temporarily or moving from one part of the country to another and being unable to get another post.

Secondly, there are some teachers who, though having taught continuously since entering the profession, for one reason or another have not taught a subject or age-range for which they were trained. Thus it might happen that they are asked to teach this 'dormant' subject or age-range, possibly to avoid redundancy or redeployment.

Thirdly, there is a large group of teachers who have occupied the same post for a considerable length of time – a period measured in decades rather than single years. Their needs, though linked to professional and academic renewal, raise the problem of motivation. How can teachers who have been doing the same job for many years be 'reinvigorated, reanimated or restored'? Meeting this area of need must present the providers of in-service education with one of their greatest challenges.

Seen as a whole, teachers' refreshment needs are very varied. And equally, in-service planned responses will have to match them in variety. For teachers re-entering the profession after a gap in service and for teachers refamiliarising themselves with the methodology of a subject or with handling a particular age-range, the experiences required of them will probably occupy short and intensive periods of in-service study. The likelihood is that these periods of work will be full-time, lasting from two weeks to perhaps half a term. Included in these blocks would be opportunities for visiting individual schools to see actual work in progress and to talk to the teachers concerned.

To meet the needs of long-serving 'static' teachers will require a much more flexible approach planned to suit the professional circumstances of the individual teacher. Where long-held attitudes, values or practices may have to be modified or brought up to date, this will not be brought about by making teachers attend crash courses or programmes[8] involving a short period of intensive full-time study. Instead what is needed is a recurring opportunity for these teachers to meet colleagues from similar schools nearby for informal discussion leading to an evaluation of existing practices and procedures. Moreover, visiting other schools in order to see how colleagues cope or to exchange jobs temporarily can also provide further professional insights. In-service patterns of study designed to meet this type of exigency will probably be 'long and thin', that is, will run for as much as a year at a time, will involve part-time release (averaging around one half-day session per week) from regular duties in school, and may include short full-time blocks of release (each lasting for about two days) to accommodate school visits. Exchange visits, which could be built into the above pattern, would be of the order of a whole term.

(4) *Teachers' Conversion Needs*
Teachers due to transfer to entirely different jobs in schools, if they have received no previous preparation for the new work may experience conversion needs. Such moves may involve external redeployment within the education service – as when a teacher initially educated for primary work is moved into a secondary school, or internal redeployment – as when a history specialist is requested to teach a shortage subject such as mathematics in the same secondary school. These cases demonstrate what can be called lateral conversion needs since teachers affected by such changes will require considerable retraining enabling them to move sideways from one post to another, their status remaining broadly unaltered.

Quite often as a result of promotion, teachers assume more weighty responsibilities and duties which are different in kind from the work that they have been doing previously. Thus a head of department may be appointed deputy head, or head be appointed adviser. The new area of responsibility is not simply an extension or widening of the old as it would be if, for example, a second in department were promoted to being head of the same department. The need experienced in a period of ante-appointment arises out of aspiration for appointment to a dissimilar kind of post. Similarly, the period before retirement or ante-retirement may be regarded as a time for in-service education when there can be preparation for life following the termination of employment in the education service. Needs like these can be described as vertical conversion needs.

To convert laterally with the aid of in-service study, especially if the latter involves learning to teach an entirely new subject-area or age-range, means that teachers have to acquire a whole body of academic knowledge, as well as its accompanying methodology (which, though not advanced, will be at B.Ed. or other first-degree level). In-service activities designed for these teachers will thus be demanding in content and time; and the likelihood is that programmes occupying anything between one term full-time (or one year part-time equivalent) and one year full-time (or two years part-time equivalent) will reflect these needs.

In contrast, to meet vertical conversion needs, in-service activities will tend to have a task-oriented and preparatory function aiming to provide the potential appointee with skills, techniques and knowledge for doing a new type of promoted job or for retirement. Ideally, the programme of study will have a sandwich pattern lasting overall for about six months. This sandwich will consist of one or two blocks of full-time study (each occupying two or three weeks during vacation time) interspersed with a series of successive study weekends during term time. At present, such ante-appointment or ante-retirement forms of in-service study for teachers are uncommon. It is more usual for teachers to be sent on courses, and so on, after appointment (and therefore making such activities part of an induction or adjustment process).

Timing of Professional Needs
Clearly some professional needs are immediate in the sense that teachers experiencing them require help at once, that is, in the short term. Examples abound in the daily work of the individual teacher – his practical organisation and discipline in classroom, workshop or laboratory; the marking of CSE coursework; or his use of reading tests. Moreover, most induction and some refreshment needs can be assumed to be immediate.

Many immediate needs may be experienced through the teacher's membership of a functional group (for instance, the need to gain certain skills or techniques in order to undertake some work in curriculum development) or as a member of the whole staff of the school (for instance, the need to digest an LEA's new policy document in advance of a staff seminar which would discuss the implications of these policies for the school).

Other needs are less-immediate, that is, they relate to the future, that is, the following term or school year. Most of the refreshment, extension and conversion needs of teachers come within this category. Help for less-immediate needs can be made available – not least because there may not be the urgency – over a greater

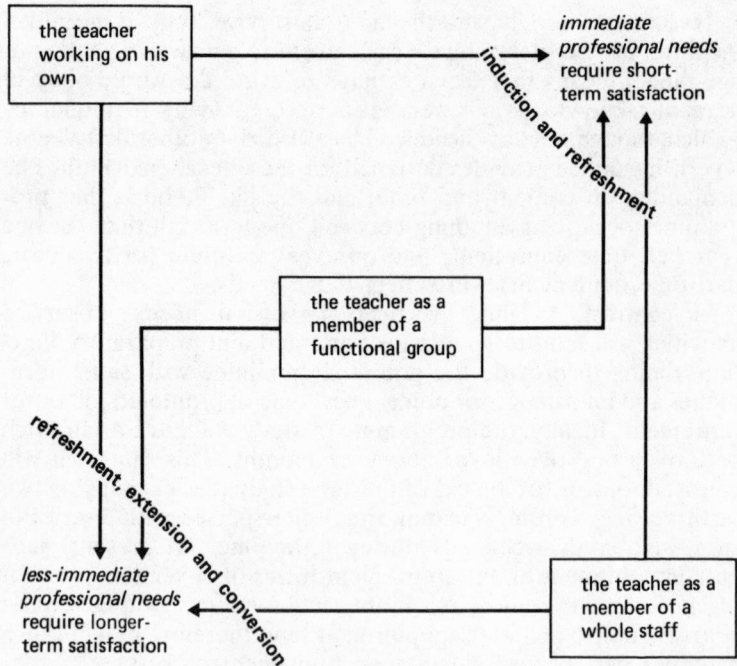

Figure 1.1 *Meeting Professional Needs*

span of time, that is, in the longer term. As with more pressing needs, these less-immediate needs can be those of the individual teacher, for instance, wishing to take an award-bearing programme the following year (extension), or the teacher as a member of a functional group or whole staff required to undertake a retraining course for teaching another subject (conversion). The relationships between professional needs and groups are indicated in Figure 1.1.

NOTES AND REFERENCES: CHAPTER 1

1 See B. Cane (1969), *In-Service Training* (Slough: NFER), p. x.
2 See James Committee (1972), *Teacher Education and Training*, Department of Education and Science report (London: HMSO), p. 5.
3 See E. S. Henderson (1978), *The Evaluation of In-Service Teacher Training* (London: Croom Helm), p. 12.
4 Said to have been coined by the late Stanley Hewitt.
5 Given in the ACSTT discussion paper, 'In-service education and training: some considerations', issued in November 1974 by the DES (mimeographed). I have taken the liberty of reversing the order of Objectives (a) and (b) to support the arguments developed in the following two paragraphs of the chapter.

6   See Department of Education and Science (1978), *Primary Education in England: A Survey by HM Inspectors of Schools* (London: HMSO).

7   This definition of induction is given in the White Paper *Education: A Framework for Expansion*, Cmnd 5174, issued by the government in 1972 (London: HMSO), p. 19.

8   Throughout this book, the composite term 'programme' is used to include all courses, conferences or other elements of provision that can be grouped naturally together as a result of planning or organisation. When courses exist in their own right as separate entities, they are referred to as such.

Chapter 2

In-Service Work
outside the School

This chapter is intended to provide a background to the general theme of the book. But it also serves the purpose of giving some essential information that should be of value when we discuss in Chapter 8 resources for the school's in-service programme. Many outside bodies have the potential of acting in a supportive capacity to the in-service work of the school. It is therefore important that teachers should know the range and nature of these external resources and how they can be called upon to assist.

A distinction is made between the different groups of outside bodies which in one way or another already provide in-service activities for teachers. Also, attention is given to the various types of in-service courses and other activities which are available, as well as to the methods by which courses – particularly when award-bearing – can be validated. Finally, there is included in this chapter a brief account of how in-service work outside schools is funded, not forgetting a brief description of financial assistance which may be made available to teachers undertaking such studies.

THE PROVIDING BODIES

Traditionally, in-service education in this country has been organised and provided outside the schools although, as will be shown, this pattern is changing. There are many different bodies, mostly public but a few private, which support teachers' in-service education. All of these bodies, some more than others, possess or have the power of deploying human and material resources for the work. In the main this traditional in-service work has consisted of long and short courses offered at universities, colleges and – more recently – teachers' centres, the purpose of which was to channel knowledge and impart skills and techniques. This method of provision has in the main conformed to a centre–periphery pattern of study diffusion, the prevailing motto of institutional providers being 'If you want it come and get it from us'.

These bodies can be divided for convenience into three groups: providing authorities, providing institutions and providing agencies.

(1) *The Providing Authorities; viz. Department of Education and Science, Local Education Authorities*

Strictly speaking, the DES is not a providing authority. The function of provision is bestowed by law on the local education authorities. However, like the LEAs the DES does arrange in-service courses for teachers, and in this respect it can be called a providing authority.

The DES organises its own annual programme of short courses,[1] each of which is residential – usually at college or university – lasting on average for three to five days. These courses, which are directed and staffed chiefly by HMIs, aim to bring together groups of teachers to discuss teaching techniques, fresh approaches to subjects taught in schools and new subject-matter. Further, it is hoped that on returning to their own localities, the teachers will be able to develop their work even more and lead conferences and courses in their neighbourhood.

Apart from this programme, the DES funds and runs jointly with university institutes and schools of education a number of regionally located courses. The patterns and duration of these DES regional courses vary considerably in keeping with local needs. Thus some of them are part-time or of sandwich type. Information about such courses is normally obtained from the appropriate institute or school of education.

The local education authorities, of which there have been 105 in England and Wales since April 1974, increasingly are making a contribution to the in-service education of teachers. This added involvement may be interpreted as a response to the James Report and the 1972 White Paper on Education, and also in terms of a heightened awareness by LEAs of their responsibility as employers of teachers. LEAs exercise their provision mainly by using members of their advisory staffs for running short courses and conferences, and in leading workshops. Moreover, local lecturers and teachers are often brought in to act as tutors for these activities which, in order to keep costs down, tend to be held on educational premises such as teachers' centres, owned or controlled by sponsoring LEAs.

Since release for teachers during working hours can obviously be arranged more easily when the employing authority happens to be the in-service provider, it is not surprising that such in-service activities do frequently occur when schools are in session.

Furthermore, these activities tend to reflect the policy requirements of parent LEAs.

(2) *The Providing Institutions*

These include those educational bodies which have a clearly
discernible corporate identity in terms of possession of academic
and non-academic staff, and control of premises, equipment and
materials, and which are responsible for teaching as the prime
function. The various institutions are:

(*a*) The universities, including the Open University;
(*b*) the polytechnics;
(*c*) the colleges and institutes of higher education;
(*d*) the colleges of education; and
(*e*) teachers' centres.

The order in which they are given is not intended to convey any
particular significance, except crudely in size.

The main drive of major providing institutions (that is, (*a*) to (*d*)
above) has always tended towards substantial and thus lengthy
forms of in-service study. However, until the Council for National
Academic Awards (CNAA) in the early 1970s took the decision to
validate award-bearing programmes of study that would be of
direct professional relevance to serving teachers, most of the
available programmes – nearly all leading to certificates, diplomas
and M.Eds – were run by universities.[2]

The position today is very different. Although the universities
including the Open University have steadily increased their stake
in the provision of award-bearing in-service programmes for
teachers, the polytechnics and colleges now also offer a wide
selection of long courses.[3] The present picture of provision is
characterised by, first, the diversity of programmes on offer,
secondly, the sharp trend towards part-time programmes in out-
of-school hours (the latter being an outcome of difficulties connected with obtaining full-time secondment), and thirdly, the large
numbers of teachers studying for their in-service B.Ed. and Open
University BA degrees.

The universities, polytechnics and colleges also run short
courses which, because they use mainly their own tutorial staff,
accommodation and other resources, tend to be self-reliant. But
the phenomenal rise of between 500 and 600 teachers' centres
in recent years, the majority of which are within close travelling
distance of where teachers work or live, has placed in-service
provision, especially of the short course type, within reach of

many teachers even in those geographical areas that are remote.

Because most centres are controlled by teacher-dominated steering committees, it follows that in-service activities offered by centres strongly reflect teachers' professional needs, centre leaders being able to make arrangements in a rapid and flexible manner. Although most centres tend to lack resources because of their small size, within the limits of their financial budgets they are able to 'buy in' tutorial support (when it is not given free) from local teachers, advisers and lecturers. Above all, teachers' centres provide a network of excellent meeting places where teachers can come together informally.

(3) *The Providing Agencies*

The agencies include a large number of disparate bodies, all with some interest or involvement in teachers' in-service education. Examples range from the Schools Council to the National Union of Teachers, or from the College of Preceptors to the Mathematical Association.

Owing to their diverse nature, it is not easy to pinpoint features that they have in common. Unlike providing authorities or institutions, agencies do not as a rule command human or physical resources for in-service work, or if they do, only on a small scale. And unlike them, agencies tend to have educational interests which are specific or sectional. Another feature of agencies is that their membership is often voluntary, depending on the payment of annual subscriptions. Hence support of in-service work by agencies tends to be centred on their specific or sectional interests and often relies for tuition on the voluntary services provided by their members. Most typical of the in-service work provided by or resulting from the initiatives of agencies is the short course, conference, summer school and teachers' workshop.

The foremost types of agency are as follows:

The subject and educational interest associations

These are too numerous to list individually. Suffice it to mention as examples of subject organisations the National Association for the Teaching of English (NATE), the Association for Science Education (ASE) and the Mathematical Association; and as examples of educational interest groups the Nursery School Association of Great Britain and Northern Ireland, the National Association for Remedial Education (NARE) and the National Association for Gifted Children.

The teachers' unions

Without exception, the unions have always claimed to exercise a professional and educational role as well as industrial role, discharging this first responsibility by organising conferences and courses for their members. In order to improve and increase this provision, the two largest unions, that is, the National Union of Teachers and the National Association of Schoolmasters/ Union of Women Teachers (NAS/UWT), have now acquired their own premises as conference centres.[4]

Apart from these, there are a small number of agencies which cannot neatly be categorised. These include the Schools Council which, it must be said, has not been prominent in the past as an in-service provider. However, with an increasing general need for information about individual projects on curriculum development, the Council is tentatively now moving into the short course and conference field. Another body is the College of Preceptors which through regional councils also runs short courses and through colleges award-bearing courses. The CNAA, though not strictly a provider in respect of the large number of long, award-bearing in-service programmes which it validates, nevertheless does occasionally initiate conferences on aspects of teacher education. And lastly, there are the broadcasting services of the BBC and IBA which are important agencies since both provide substantial coverage for in-service work via the media of television and radio.

IN-SERVICE ACTIVITIES

This review of external provision would be incomplete without mention of the variety of forms of study that may be experienced by teachers. Allowing for the fact that the list might not be all-embracing, these forms could include:

Formal lecture
Plenary session at conference
Demonstration
Individual or group practical work in laboratory, workshop or
    classroom
Distance learning, for example by correspondence course
TV or radio instructional session
Teachers' 'work-in' or workshop
Informal discussion
Teach-ins
Visits to schools and to other teachers
Teacher exchanges
Group and individual tutorials
Seminars

Syndicates, that is, problem-solving groups
Group and individual counselling/guidance sessions
Programmed learning
Private study and practice
Interviews
Guided individual reading
Structured observing
Investigative sessions in library
Sessions with an internal or external consultant.

These study activities, with the possible exception of visits involving teachers and schools, are not exclusively characteristic of in-service education. They may serve as 'one-off' activities or be grouped in suitable combinations, according to the needs of the learning situation, to construct any of the following patterns of study:

(1) Major programmes leading to the award of diplomas, first degrees (such as the in-service B.Ed.) and higher degrees.
(2) Long courses leading to other in-service qualifications, such as post-experience certificates.
(3) Short courses and short sandwich courses, normally non award-bearing.
(4) Conferences organised at national, regional and local levels.
(5) Small-scale educational research which may, though not invariably, lead to award of a higher degree.
(6) Educational travel or visits abroad, for example involving teacher exchanges for, say, a year at a time.
(7) Engagement, possibly on secondment, in curriculum development project work at national, regional or local level.
(8) Secondment to industry and social services.
(9) In-service work involving groups of professionally related, or geographically adjacent, schools, for example belonging to an in-service consortium or sharing the same campus.
(10) Schoolteacher fellowships or associateships at universities and colleges.
(11) Secondment on totally independent study, for example at the behest of the individual teacher's LEA.

Looking at this list of patterns of study, it can be taken for granted that some of these patterns are far more frequently pursued by teachers as students than others. Up-to-date evidence is hard to come by, but in terms of gross numbers enrolled the most popular patterns would appear to be short courses and conferences, while award-bearing programmes and courses would probably not figure highly on the list, no doubt due to the inability of teachers to be granted secondment.

In a DES national survey[5] it was discovered that in the year 1977–8 305,000 teachers (that is, between 60 and 70 per cent of those in regular service in England and Wales) participated in in-service work. Of this surprisingly high total, 170,000 teachers took part in studies which did not require release from normal classroom duties (defined in the survey as absence over and above a teacher's normal non-teaching periods) and 135,000 did require release. Of the latter, slightly more than 2,000 were seconded full-time for a term or longer, leaving 133,000 on other full-time or part-time modes of study.

Discounting these 2,000 secondments, the survey found that the average release period was $3\frac{1}{2}$ days for the year. Furthermore, since just over 13,000 teachers (that is, 2.9 per cent of all teachers in regular service) were following long courses leading to awards, one firm conclusion is that by far the larger proportion of in-service work consists of brief activities. What we do not know – and certainly it cannot be deduced from the survey – is the actual proportion of 303,000 teachers (which, incidentally, did not include probationers) who were taking part in in-service activities *at* their schools during or after working hours or in external activities at the request of their schools.

Many of the other patterns of study which may be occasionally practised, such as secondment to industry or taking up school-teacher fellowships, will have to await new national policies heralding a significant upturn in in-service education before they come into their own.

COURSE VALIDATION

An important function of in-service providers is to ensure that their programmes and courses meet certain explicitly accepted standards, not least for ensuring that criticism from teachers undertaking study is reduced to a minimum. Validation is a powerful tool which is available to validators for establishing in the first place such standards and for maintaining them thereafter. So what do we. mean by validation?

It is the process by which programmes and courses, initiated by providing institutions and other bodies, may be judged sound or well-grounded in terms of widely accepted criteria, of which the two most important in the context of in-service education are academic standard and professional relevance.

Validation, a form of evaluation, not only safeguards consumers' interests, but in ensuring the general acceptability of the programme or course to society at large, it helps to guarantee the integrity and credibility of the providing body (or bodies) and underwrites the quality of any award that may be ultimately conferred on successful students.

Every providing body, whether authority, institution or agency, thus has a responsibility to take all necessary action to validate those programmes or courses for which it is immediately responsible, that is, for planning the work and providing the tuition. This type of validation carried out by the providing body's own staff during the period when programmes and courses are being developed or reviewed is known as internal validation. Moreover, some providing bodies, chiefly the universities, possess a considerable degree of administrative and academic autonomy, often derived from a charter conferred by the Crown in Privy Council. Such bodies may be said to practise self-validation when they develop programmes and courses, provide tuition and other resources for these activities, and confer awards.

Some colleges and polytechnics too are self-validating in respect of some kinds of in-service programmes and courses for which they offer their own certificates and, sometimes, diplomas. In theory there is nothing to prevent any providing body, even as small as a teachers' centre or self-regulating consortium of schools, from exercising freedom to act in this manner, save the knowledge that acceptance of such awards in the eyes of outsiders – teacher-consumers, LEA employers or the public at large – might be hard to win.

Another procedure frequently occurring is for a college or polytechnic's internal validation to be underwritten by external validation supplied by a second body. In this situation, the first institution's programmes or courses will be subjected to rigorous academic and professional scrutiny by staff of the second institution. This kind of validation is afforded in this country by some though by no means all universities, the CNAA and a small number of subject associations (notably the Mathematical Association, and through their Joint Board the Library Association and School Library Association). Technically, external validation does not have to be linked to award of qualifications: a providing institution could award its own certificate or other qualification which was externally validated. In practice, however, the prestige and academic reputation of the external validator makes conferment of a qualification in the name of that validator a more compelling proposition.

Of all the external validators, the CNAA now stands well above every university as the chief body in the United Kingdom for validating programmes of study leading to qualifications in initial and in-service teacher education. Yet, strangely, it is an organisation of which teachers often have little knowledge.

Established by royal charter in 1964, the CNAA rapidly assumed its pre-eminent position today as the main external validator for colleges and polytechnics in the public sector of higher education. The CNAA is not a university but the programmes of study that it validates and the qualifications which it bestows are nevertheless equivalent to those offered by British universities. The Council has a small full-time staff whose job is to facilitate consideration of proposals submitted by individual institutions. The crucial task of programme and course vetting and approval is undertaken by panels of unpaid members of staff of universities, colleges and polytechnics, all of whom are experts in their own fields of study and who wish to support the work of the Council.

To complete this picture of validation, mention should be made of what may be described as institutional recognition or accreditation which in the narrow sense is not validation as it does not involve programme development on the part of client institutions. Thus an awarding body (such as the University of London in respect of its external degrees, the College of Preceptors or the City and Guilds Institute) may contract out the teaching of a programme or course to a suitably resourced providing institution, sometimes because the awarding body does not possess appropriate teaching resources itself. In such a situation, the institution undertaking the actual tuition can be perceived as fulfilling a servicing function on behalf of the awarding body.

Though the London University external degree system which has for many years provided for teachers a major in-service route leading to award-bearing qualifications is being phased out, the College of Preceptors through accredited institutions will continue to offer its range of qualifications. Indeed the College is now extending its involvement in teachers' in-service education and has recently entered the field of external validation in respect of one of its Alternative Schemes for the ACP (described in the Directory of Resources).

FUNDING OF IN-SERVICE WORK

The financing of in-service education is complex. Though it is difficult to outline in a few paragraphs, here is the gist of it. If first we consider the cost of providing in-service activities, there are several sources from which money can be obtained for this purpose:

(1) In those providing institutions maintained by local education authorities (chiefly colleges of higher education and polytechnics), the parent authorities are empowered to charge some of the cost of approved courses[6] lasting four weeks or more full-time (or the part-time equivalent) to the advanced further education pool.[7] The rest of the cost is met from the rates.

(2) In the case of non-approved (and thus non-poolable) courses – usually short courses or conferences, and so on, run by advisers or teachers' centres – the full cost is met by the LEAs from the rates.

(3) In voluntary institutions of higher education (mostly church colleges) the cost of in-service work generally is included in the total annual grant paid by the DES for maintaining these institutions.

(4) In universities, the cost of all in-service work is included in the total quinquennial grant for funding all activities received from the University Grants Committee (UGC).

The cost of providing courses and other patterns of study in these various institutions is normally determined after taking into account income received from tuition fees.

Another major element of expenditure in calculating the total cost of in-service education is that of the salaries of teachers released. For those fortunate enough to obtain full-time secondment, employing authorities are permitted to claim back from the pool 75 per cent of salaries in order to enable them to pursue approved courses of four weeks or more. The significance of this procedure is that it allows LEAs to meet the cost of temporarily replacing in school the teachers that have been seconded. A major criticism, however, is that LEAs are not permitted to recoup such costs in respect of equivalent part-time courses (lasting, say, for half a day per week for a year) whether held in or out of school-time.

Teachers attending full- or part-time patterns of study may receive financial assistance from their employing authorities. This can include tuition and registration fees, travelling expenses, and maintenance including accommodation costs. In the case of approved full-time courses (again of four weeks or more in length) and equivalent part-time courses, LEAs are permitted to recover 100 per cent of this expenditure from the pool.

A useful summary of the procedures that teachers should follow in applying for financial assistance when wishing to enrol for poolable courses is given in the DES handbook of long courses published annually which outlines the full programme. In 'Notes for Applicants' given as an introduction to the booklet are also included sections dealing with eligibility for secondment, making application, superannuation and pension rights. All these should be referred to by intending students.

NOTES AND REFERENCES: CHAPTER 2

1 These are listed in a handbook published annually by the Department of Education and Science jointly with the Welsh Office Education Department, entitled *Short Courses for Teachers*, which is distributed free to schools and other educational establishments.

2 See DES Statistics Division (1970), 'Courses provided in the period 1st September, 1966, to 31st August, 1967', which is to be found in Department of Education and Science (1970), *Survey of In-Service Training for Teachers, 1967*, Statistics of Education – Special Series No. 2 (London: HMSO), p. 26.

3 Listed in the DES and Welsh Office Education Department's annual handbook *Long Courses for Qualified Teachers*, which is distributed free to schools and colleges.

4 The NUT Conference Centre is at Stoke Rochford Hall, Grantham, Lincs., and the NAS/UWT Hillscourt Education Centre is at Rose Hill, Rednal, Birmingham.

5 See Department of Education and Science (1978), 'Induction and in-service training of teachers: 1978 survey', *Statistical Bulletin*, issue 8/78.

6 An 'approved course' is any pattern of study recognised by the DES and listed in its annual programme of long courses (see note 3 above).

7 The 'pool' is the mechanism whereby public sector higher education is financed. It covers most of the work leading to degrees, diplomas, and so on, undertaken by polytechnics and colleges of education or higher education. All LEAs contribute to this cost via the pool so that those LEAs which actually maintain institutions of higher education do not have to bear all the cost themselves.

Chapter 3

The School and In-Service Education

An explanation is given in this chapter as to how in-service education has evolved down to the present time and why it has come under recent criticism. This leads to consideration of the school as a suitable base for in-service work. The chapter concludes with a description of some reported instances of schools running their own in-service programmes of study.

AN EVOLVING IN-SERVICE PICTURE

To understand how in-service education in England and Wales has developed in the last hundred or so years, that is, since the advent of popular education, it is necessary to look at the path which initial teacher education has taken during this time. Before 1856 teachers received one year's training at college, but from then on until 1962 the large majority of qualified teachers – and there were many unqualified teachers also serving in schools during this period – undertook a two-year course of initial training leading to the award of the teachers' certificate in education. Moreover, immediately after the Second World War a large number of ex-military personnel entered the profession by means of the one-year emergency training scheme in order to overcome the severe shortage of teachers caused by the hostilities.

More recent landmarks in initial teacher education have been the emergence since 1963 of the three-year programme of training for certificated teachers and, since 1968, of the four-year B.Ed. degree programme. More recently, the decision has been taken to phase out completely certificate programmes. Thus from 1982 onwards, nearly all newly qualified teachers entering schools will possess either a B.Ed. degree gained in three or four years or another first degree plus the postgraduate certificate in education.

This slight detour underlines the fact that until as recently as the 1960s the teaching profession was not particularly well educated when compared with the other great professions such as medicine or dentistry. Even as late as 1977, according to the Green Paper[1] on Education, just under three-quarters of all teachers in service were non-graduate (that is, certificated) and of these, about half (150,000) were two-year educated.

In the last hundred years there has gradually developed a practice of taking teachers out of their schools and providing them, as Euan Henderson[2] says, with in-service courses to upgrade their basic education (the 'top-up' approach). That this policy has been reaffirmed and catered for in the last fifteen or so years is illustrated by the number of one-year and one-term full-time supplementary courses that have been offered to two-year certificated teachers since 1963. Indeed, in recent years the introduction of programmes of study for two- or three-year certificate-holders leading to the in-service B.Ed. degree may be regarded as another manifestation of this prevailing 'top-up' policy for in-service education.

Henderson argues that the external course-based model of in-service education from the early years of this century expanded its function from a means of upgrading to a means of teaching teachers everything they may need to know. In-service education as traditionally provided thus became a panacea for professional development and, by implication, for improving the quality of schools and the education of children. He suggests that for quite a long time, there has been an uncritical acceptance of the need for more in-service courses of the traditional type, an acceptance especially by official committees on education (for example, Newsom, Plowden, Gittings). And he observes that, though the expansion of this form of education has been 'near-exponential' and has built up into a very expensive industry, little has been done until very recently to find out whether this type of in-service education achieves worthwhile results.

It is axiomatic that the purpose of any type of in-service education – irrespective of whether it takes place in universities, colleges or elsewhere and whatever its length – is intended to make the practising teacher better at performing his job. Thus after completing his studies and resuming his duties in school, there ought to be some tangible evidence that what he has learnt and will now be attempting to apply within his class- or subject-room will be of direct professional value to himself and his colleagues. And yet one of the chief criticisms of external types of in-service education is that, more often than not, the actual benefits to the school, if not to the teacher, are minimal.

Why is this so? There are two connected reasons frequently advanced, the first being the manner in which in-service patterns of study are often planned and introduced. Many of these activities are brought into being by providing institutions which fail to pay enough attention to the needs of schools and the teachers who serve in them. As a consequence, externally designed activities tend to be susceptible to the charge that they are irrelevant to the real needs of teachers or that they are too theoretical.

The companion reason derives from a general failure in the education service – of which no group whether of administrators, lecturers or teachers can escape blame – to acknowledge that schools should be accepted as central to many of the decision-making processes affecting in-service education rather than peripheral. As a result, teachers often enrol for courses on a hit-or-miss basis without being led to understand in advance the suitability or relevance of their proposed studies. Rarely do schools play a significant role in counselling or preparing teachers before they embark on study so that such individuals can obtain the maximum benefit from their impending labours. Neither do schools systematically 'debrief' their teachers upon their return after courses have been completed in order that the newly attained expertise may be brought to the attention and interest of the wider audience of the staff. Sometimes a school's failure to capitalise on these in-service resources obtained externally can be interpreted as a 'sin of commission', as for example when the staff come to regard their colleague's new-found skills or knowledge as a threat to time-honoured methods used in the classroom (that is, to the 'real' work going on at the 'chalkface'). At other times a staff's collective attitude may be understood as a 'sin of omission', when for instance they regard the newly acquired resource with total indifference.

The recent development of techniques for evaluating in-service education by Euan Henderson[3] and others should be of assistance henceforth in substantiating or refuting criticisms of this kind and enable the providers on the one hand and the customers or clients on the other to make more informed professional judgements.

Also the establishment in the last few years of in-service consultative or advisory committees by most polytechnics and colleges on which teachers are strongly represented can do much to improve the lines of communication, especially when new patterns of study are being proposed. College tutors therefore have less excuse than formerly of not knowing what teachers want.

THE SCHOOL AS A BASE FOR IN-SERVICE WORK

Our next task is to consider the concept of in-service work generated within the school itself, in part a reaction and response to the criticisms indicated above. Of course the reader may hardly need reminding that a good deal of in-service work has been going on in schools for a long time:

The guidance given to the probationer on how to control Form 4X.

The lengthy briefing by the headteacher of his deputy heads following a reallocation of senior management duties in a comprehensive school.

The assistance forthcoming from an experienced science teacher to a less experienced colleague on setting up some new apparatus in a laboratory.

The advice given by an older teacher to a younger teacher on how to handle a particularly difficult child.

All these are illustrative of the day-to-day help that staff colleagues give each other. Thus the notion of in-service education in school, albeit organised informally and probably not recognised as in-service work, is one that has been practised for a long time.

But what is new is the recognition in many educational quarters that in-service education in the school sphere can be planned and pursued on a formal basis. It is this approach which deserves attention and which will now be examined in detail.

To imagine in-service education in school without qualification would leave us with a hazy understanding of what was implied. Our perception is sharpened if the work in its most self-reliant form is assumed to include all of the following features:

(1) It would serve the school's institutional and, therefore, educational needs.
(2) It would be intended for teachers actually serving at the school.
(3) It would be initiated and planned by members of the school staff.
(4) It would be led and executed by members of the school staff.
(5) It would utilise the school's physical resources.
(6) It would take place on the school premises.

There have been a number of reports of schools running their own programmes of in-service education. But hardly any of these reports reflect the above model closely and none reflects it entirely. The accounts nearly all involve comprehensive schools. The programmes are probably a response to a need for finding solutions to the problems and challenges following secondary reorganisation. These summaries are given in the order in which the reports were originally published.

Thomas Calton School, Peckham
The school was faced, according to Ron Pepper,[4] the headmaster, with having to move into new, purpose-built buildings (which in the event were not forthcoming). The staff took the decision that a programme of in-service education would be needed as a preparation for this change. Because of the practical difficulty of releasing teachers during the working day in order to attend external sessions at local teachers' centres, college of education, and so on, it was agreed that the programme should consist of school-based training sessions involving 'learning within one's own teaching environment'.

Encouraged by the LEA, the staff identified four main areas of need, initiating the following programme to meet them:

(1) The use of audio-visual equipment: Sessions were undertaken in school in out-of-school hours and were led by visiting teachers. The school's own media resources officer also gave assistance in learning to use equipment.

(2) Development of team teaching and integrated studies: Planning started with a general meeting of all staff who were interested. This led to the formation of a working group to hammer out a draft statement of aims and objectives. Outside speakers were invited to give their ideas and suggest approaches. Once agreement had been reached, volunteers for year teams – starting with Years 1 and 2 – were called for which met weekly to work out a series of themes and topics, to prepare materials and to timetable the operation.

(3) Visits to other schools: It was considered necessary that to prepare for integration and team teaching, an examination of what other schools were doing to cope with change should take place. Thus it became possible to close the school for half a day in order to visit a neighbouring school and study the latter's non-streamed approach. This was preceded by a preliminary visit involving informal departmental discussions and was followed by further discussions.

(4) Co-ordination and communication: A staff bulletin was issued at fortnightly intervals carrying reports of meetings and group activities, articles from members of staff and press cuttings of outside developments. A new post, co-ordinator of studies, was created to ensure that all aspects of the school's developmental work were co-ordinated, that resources were not

unnecessarily duplicated, that real needs were identified, and that the communication system was unclogged and two-way. Also, the co-ordinator's task was to keep the school's in-service programme moving.

Benfield Comprehensive School, Newcastle upon Tyne
Robert Martin[5] describes how a decision was taken to change the existing banded system operating at the school by allocating part of the new ten-form intake of pupils at 11-plus to mixed ability forms as an attempt to find a more efficient learning system. It was recognised from the outset that for mixed ability teaching to last sufficiently long for it to be tested thoroughly, not only would staff support for the introduction of mixed ability grouping be needed but the staff would need time to prepare for the actual changeover. The in-service programme which was initiated was developed as a response to these needs. It was phased over the school year to support and keep in step with the prerequisite changes that were necessary to implement mixed ability grouping and teaching.

Policy in the school was determined by the joint committee consisting of senior administrative, academic and tutorial staff. In September, the committee took the decision to introduce mixed ability grouping the following year. This was followed by making available photocopied summaries of publications dealing with the subject to heads of department for discussion with their colleagues. During the first two terms of the year, three in-service activities were reported as taking place:

(1) Guest speakers with experience of mixed ability work came to the school to lecture the staff.
(2) Some members of staff visited other schools where mixed ability grouping had been introduced.
(3) Also, several members of staff attended an external course, 'Teaching Unstreamed Classes', and then reported back to the joint committee on their experiences.

By Easter, the joint committee decided that two forms (of the ten-form entry) would be mixed ability in the following September. This decision enabled the subject departments to use the summer term in completing their detailed preparations and for parents to be informed of the intended changes.

Norton Priory Comprehensive School, Runcorn
Unlike the in-service programmes of the above two schools, the length of which can be measured in months if not years, the Norton Priory programme consisted of a two-and-a-half day staff

conference which was held, not on the school premises, but at the Hydro Hotel, Llandudno. Details of this conference, given by David Warwick[6] in his book, exemplify the type of in-service activity pioneered by the Cheshire LEA on behalf of its comprehensive schools.

The general purpose of the conference was to outline new educational policy and to relate it to each section of the school. Several visiting speakers were invited to give key lectures to the staff, and afterwards each subject or theme was discussed by members divided into groups. These included mixed ability teaching, the integrated curriculum, counselling and guidance, and the community school.

Ashmead School, Reading
In his book Lawrence Stenhouse[7] describes how the headmaster, Peter Judge, built school-based training into the formal structure of the school by appointing a training deputy head. The description is of particular interest here because it concentrates attention on roles and structures in respect of in-service education in school rather than activities or subjects of study.

Stenhouse reproduces the job specification for the training deputy head, namely:

(1) The organising of teaching practice
(2) The forging of links with the local college and university
(3) The supervision of probationary teachers
(4) The arranging of internally and externally located courses for existing school staff
(5) The counselling of all staff with problems
(6) The arranging of all interviews for new appointments in consultation with the head and heads of department
(7) The induction of all new arrivals
(8) The introduction of regular job appraisal sessions and the training of senior staff in their use
(9) The regular appraisal of inter-staff communications and suggestions for improvements
(10) Liaison with the curriculum development centre.

When appointed, the holder of this post worked through an in-service training committee. Membership of the committee of which he was chairman included a year head with counselling skills, a young teacher with links to staff discussion groups, a probationer designated annually, an experienced teacher, a mid-career teacher with specialised careers knowledge, and a head of department involved in curriculum training problems.

The committee had four functions. These were:

(1) to propose and design support for individual teachers, chiefly by defining roles and in providing school-based courses and other forms of training;
(2) to analyse and recommend appropriate changes in respect of school organisation;
(3) to assist in staff welfare;
(4) to support ongoing curriculum development in the school, by reviewing progress and in disseminating information on discrete elements of work to the rest of the staff.

Reporting to the governors on one year's programme of in-service work at the school, the training deputy head commented that the basic problem was that of reconciling the process of fundamental organisational changes with the more complex difficulties of human adjustment that inevitably follow.

Rivington and Blackrod High School, Bolton

Like the in-service programmes of other schools, this was developed as a response to perceived needs of the staff following secondary reorganisation. It is described in an article written by the headmaster, Ronald Fell,[8] who indicates that a main requirement was to construct a stock of resource materials (to be held in two resource centres) which could be used to support mixed ability grouping in Years 1 to 3 in the school. Thus an in-service programme was designed to train staff to become competent and knowledgeable in furthering these innovations.

Fell lists several objectives for the programme. Broadly, these cover:

(1) becoming proficient in constructing resource materials;
(2) learning to use a storage and retrieval system within a resource centre;
(3) understanding the underlying educational principles of resource-based learning; and
(4) examining the wider educational and organisational questions connected with curriculum innovation in the school.

The programme consisted of a number of separate self-contained short courses repeated at regular intervals. Each course occupied a Friday and Monday, allowing staff to work out their ideas at leisure over the weekend. Three teachers, each from a different faculty, comprised the membership of a course-run, the opportunity of inter-faculty discussion being stressed as an important side-effect of the work.

The structure of each course was that Day 1 would be given over to theoretical and descriptive contributions supplied by the head-master, the head of creative studies, the assistant head responsible for curriculum and resources, and the director of resources. Day 2 would commence with a contribution by the school librarian, and the rest of the time would be spent by the teachers working on their own resource project. The day would conclude with a short evaluation session led by the headmaster.

Hartcliffe School, Bristol
Anita Ellis[9] reports on an in-service course run for fifty-seven members of staff concerned with pastoral care and the social education of its pupils. She mentions that the course was one of four projects contributing to an overall programme of in-service education designed for the staff. The other three comprised:

(1) two residential weekend sessions under direction of the head when twenty-three senior staff considered the task of the school, its actual needs, its policy framework and the overall curriculum;
(2) a day conference when the whole staff considered the basic objectives of the school by means of small-group discussions (interestingly, this included a cross-section of former pupils who had left three or four years before); and
(3) a day conference when the humanities faculty of thirty teachers considered the implications of the relationship between teacher and pupils as being itself part of the cur-riculum.

The course on pastoral care and social education was initiated by Anita Ellis who had responsibility at the school for staff development. The course arose out of a need among the staff to examine fundamentally the task and role of tutor. The LEA agreed to support the course financially and the local branch of the National Marriage Guidance Council accepted an invitation to become involved in the project.

The course consisted of three phases. In the first one the fifty-seven teachers were put into heterogeneous groups of approx-imately ten members each. These represented different levels of status and role, and different ideological positions, and were mixed by age and sex. The groups' task was to look at the individual child within his group tutor context and to become more sensitised to his tutor group's behaviour. In the second phase, the teachers were given the opportunity of exploring, with external professionals, resources outside the school and for learning how best to use them.

The third phase consisted of a residential weekend attended by twenty of the original fifty-seven. Its purpose was to help the staff groups explore their feelings and behaviour in the 'here and now' situation and to learn from these experiences.

Chesterton School, Cambridge

In an account of in-service work at Chesterton School, an 11 to 16 comprehensive, Hugh Wood[10] describes how a school-based course was run in the academic year 1977–8. What makes the account particularly noteworthy is that the course was run by Dr Charles Bailey of Homerton College and counted for the award of the Certificate of Further Professional Study from Cambridge Institute of Education.

Mr Wood at the time was assistant headmaster of the school, having a brief for staff development and the organisation of in-service work among the teachers. His links with Homerton were strong since he had previously served there as a lecturer, and this fact clearly was an important factor in his being able to pursue the idea of a school-based award-bearing in-service course.

The content of the course was not decided in advance, or exclusively, by the college. Instead, there was plenty of discussion among those members of staff who thought a school-based course a good idea. This led to mutual identification by the school and college of suitable topics for study within the general area of curriculum studies.

Most of the meetings were held on the school premises during the 'twilight' period from 4.00 to 5.30 p.m. on Wednesdays. In addition to these meetings, sixteen altogether, there were three Saturday morning sessions at school and a whole-day conference at college. These additional sessions added variety and allowed time for more sustained study.

Although many of the sessions of study involved college tutors who introduced and led aspects of the syllabus, there was an emphasis on discussion rather than on mere note-taking. Many of the later sessions in the year included the presentation of seminar papers by course members. Apart from the requirement that members should attend 80 per cent of the sessions, assessment was based on written coursework deriving from preparation of these seminar papers.

Of eighteen members (25 per cent of the total staff of the school) who commenced the course, fifteen eventually completed it and obtained the certificate.

Hugh Wood completes his account by indicating the advantages and disadvantages of the school-based course:

(1) Participation as course members in the work, for example in discussion, took place rapidly as everyone knew each other from the start.
(2) Since all members tended to identify with the aims and methods of the school, this unanimity of view detracted from good argument.
(3) The general level of awareness and concern in the school was raised through informal discussion taking place in the staffroom and elsewhere resulting from issues raised in the course.

It became apparent towards the end of the year that the course had created new opportunities not least because members in future wanted to become more involved in decision-making on the curriculum of the school. In the subsequent year, therefore, further work of a follow-up nature was done bringing about a number of curriculum changes.

Heathland School, Hounslow
In describing this school-based programme, Geoffrey Samuel,[11] the head, says that it should include the three areas of initial training, induction and in-service training.

Overall responsibility rested with a senior member of staff called the professional tutor who had staff development in her brief. Significantly, Samuel comments that to have a 'counselling' attitude to the work would be totally incompatible with the role of training officer (which the role of professional tutor was at Heathland School).

Much of the professional tutor's work was to make arrangements for students' teaching practice and the induction of probationers. Thus she developed contacts with external bodies such as a local college of education which invited her to act as a visiting tutor, and neighbouring schools which probationers were given the opportunity to visit.

In the article, Samuel develops in some detail the relationship between the professional tutor and heads of department. Accepting that detailed and day-to-day help for guiding probationers should rest with heads of department, the school adopted the position that the professional tutor would give advice to heads, in particular laying down guidelines for the topics to be covered in discussion between heads of department and their newly qualified teachers.

An important function of the professional tutor was with the head of the school to inspect probationers' lessons. There were two periods of inspection, one at the beginning and the other at the end of the induction year. On the basis of reports made on these and others submitted by heads of department, consolidated reports were sent to the LEA.

The article concludes by describing other in-service activities taking place at the school. These included:

(1) departments arranging their own in-service work;
(2) an annual half-day course for heads of department; and
(3) a programme of in-service work for all the pastoral staff organised by a deputy head, bringing in outside agencies such as the school psychological service.

The professional tutor was expected to keep detailed information about this work, to encourage staff to take part and to arrange for reports to be written on it.

Moons Moat Nursery and First School
In possibly the only primary school account available, Mrs Simmons,[12] the headmistress, describes a programme of school-based in-service education which was set in the context of staff development of which the suggested aims were:

(1) Improvement in current performance and remediation of existing weaknesses.
(2) Preparation of staff for changing duties and responsibilities.
(3) Enhancement of job satisfaction.
(4) Preparation of teachers for advancement, either within their present school or elsewhere.

The first task of the head and her colleagues in bringing about such staff development was to identify their training needs. Resulting from this, priority was assigned to the areas of behaviour modification, language, reading and mathematics; while other areas covering most aspects of the curriculum were named at later stages.

The programme of work was based from the outset on a system of regular seminars. These were held after school and dealt with one topic at a time. The teacher in charge of the area of the curriculum normally led the seminar, and this involved conducting discussion, arranging subsequent meetings, making notes and finally producing a written report which was intended to form the basis of future teaching in that area.

Taking turns in leading seminars, teachers soon overcame their trepidation and developed powers of leadership, confidence and self-esteem as well as organisational and presentational skills.

It was found that in some areas the combined inputs of the staff were inadequate, and it became necessary to obtain outside assistance from an LEA inspector and two tutors from a local college of further education.

A product of the seminar system was for the teacher responsible in the school for mathematics to hold a one-hour 'surgery' every Tuesday after lessons when she was available for consultation by staff colleagues.

One particular contribution made by the head to staff development was to assist senior colleagues for promotion by giving them training in staff selection and interviewing procedures, and in discussing case-study material.

The intellectual development of the teachers was helped by encouraging each member of staff in turn to buy a book out of school funds for the staff library. The individual choosing the book had the duty of reading it and presenting a résumé of its contents to the rest of the staff. The head reinforced this by providing the teachers with relevant DES publications and 'newsy' articles which stimulated more discussion and sharing of opinions.

The report of Mrs Simmons ends by mentioning four measures by which evaluation of the progress of the teachers undertaking the in-service education was carried out. These were:

(1) Subjective assessment of the teachers by the head in which there was a system of half-yearly staff appraisal interviews each lasting an hour.
(2) Continuous appraisal of colleagues by teachers with curricular responsibilities.
(3) Obtaining evidence that school-based in-service education was stimulating teachers to enrol on external courses, for instance with the Open University.
(4) Hope for improvement in standards, increased job satisfaction and a willingness to accept extra responsibility.

Some Comments on These Nine Reports
In matching a school's actual experiences with the 'self-reliant' model of in-service education based on the school, it is evident that the school which corresponds most closely is that of Rivington and Blackrod. The head of this school gave four objectives for the programme which were related to a narrow range of professional needs connected with constructing a stock of resource materials, and so on. It was therefore fairly straightforward for the staff to

plan a simple programme of work that could rely on its own teaching resources. There is no evidence in the report that external resources were brought in to reinforce the teachers' total contribution or that individual members of staff were sent elsewhere to obtain new knowledge, skills or experiences.

However, there were several schools that identified a much broader range of professional needs and decided to put in motion a more ambitious programme of in-service education than that at Rivington and Blackrod. Examples of such schools were Thomas Calton, Ashmead and Hartcliffe. These schools in particular found that they lacked the range and variety of internal resources to support the work and they thus found that in order to meet specific in-service objectives, they had to bring in outside people who possessed appropriate experiences to lead sessions, or they had to send members of staff on external courses or to other schools.

It is true that nearly all the schools decided on in-service programmes that were intended to meet the perceived professional needs of individual members of the respective staffs. The school that devised a programme of in-service education that was explicitly linked to a comprehensive pattern of staff development was Moons Moat. This policy dictated that the work had to adapt closely in meeting some of the more personal needs of the teachers, for instance in equipping them to take additional responsibility in the school or for promotion. Although self-reliant in many aspects of its in-service education, the school encouraged its teachers to draw on external support when necessary.

There were two schools which appeared to take part in in-service activities that were not closely tailored to the professional needs of the actual staff. One was Chesterton which partly adapted an external award-bearing course to its own use. The same seems to be the case for Norton Priory which according to the report accepted an externally determined pattern of study in the form of a conference provided for this and other schools by its LEA. Furthermore, the programme depended to a great extent on inputs from outside speakers; little came from the school's own resources. Thus for both these schools, the educational experiences were neither self-reliant, nor were they matched precisely to individual teachers' needs.

One concluding comment: a lack of self-reliance in a school's programme does not necessarily constitute a criticism; however, to mismatch in-service experiences to the needs of individual teachers does, and it is the resolution of this problem that we shall be attending to in the next and subsequent chapters.

NOTES AND REFERENCES: CHAPTER 3

1 Given in Department of Education and Science (1977), *Education in Schools: A Consultative Document*, Green Paper (London: HMSO), p. 25.
2 See E. Henderson (1979), 'The concept of school-focussed in-service education and training', *British Journal of Teacher Education*, vol. 5, No. 1, p. 18.
3 E. Henderson (1978), *The Evaluation of In-Service Teacher Training* (London: Croom Helm).
4 R. Pepper (1972), 'In-service training and the Thomas Calton School, Peckham', *Forum*, vol. 14, no. 2, pp. 50–2.
5 R. Martin (1973), 'Mixed ability in a comprehensive school', *Secondary Education*, vol. 4, no. 1, pp. 7–10.
6 D. Warwick (1975), *School-Based In-Service Education* (Edinburgh: Oliver & Boyd), ch. 6, pp. 37–8.
7 L. Stenhouse (1975), *An Introduction to Curriculum Research and Development* (London: Heinemann), ch. 11, pp. 166–80.
8 R. Fell (1976), 'In-service training', *General Education*, spring no., pp. 26–9.
9 A. Ellis (1976), 'In-school in-service training for tutors', *British Journal of Guidance and Counselling*, vol. 4, no. 2, pp. 218–23.
10 H. Wood (1979), 'The Chesterton school-based in-service course', *Cambridge Journal of Education*, vol. 9, nos 2 and 3, pp. 128–35.
11 G. Samuel (1980), 'School-based INSET in action', *Education*, vol. 155, no. 5, p. 120.
12 L. M. Simmons (1980), 'Staff development in schools', *Curriculum*, vol. 1, no. 1, pp. 10–14.

Chapter 4

The School-Focused Approach

During the last few years the term 'school-based in-service education' has become part of our educational jargon. What is it? How
does the 'school-focused' approach differ from it? Or do they
really mean the same thing? Answers to questions about these and
other, closely related, concepts are proffered in this chapter. The
latter concludes with some examples of ways in which various
kinds of schools – from infant schools to sixth form colleges – can
provide school-focused in-service education and make use of
resources, particularly from outside, for this purpose.

SOME ALLIED CONCEPTS AND THEIR DISTINCTION

It has already been mentioned that the traditional policy for
teachers' in-service education has been to provide external, off-
the-job courses located on campuses of colleges, universities,
teachers' centres, and so on. An alternative which is only now
becoming widespread is to provide in-service work at school, that
is, on the school premises or on-the-job. This notion of school-
based in-service education has been seen in some quarters as
meaning courses or other in-service activities provided for
teachers using the accommodation of the school where they are
employed.

It is undoubtedly true that many external providers of in-service
courses have good reason for using school premises: for instance,
an LEA modern languages adviser might wish to have access to a
language laboratory in a conveniently located school for a French
short course; or the leader of a teachers' centre might arrange for
appropriate facilities in a school to be put at the disposal of a group
of primary teachers wanting to make simple scientific apparatus.
Such activities are as a general rule given wide publicity and are
made available to teachers from more than one school. Though
literally school-based, in-service work such as this is not exclusively designed for assisting the professional needs of the staff of
the host school. Rather the general position is to employ the term

'school-based' to described the kind of in-service activity that is run on the school premises for the sole benefit of the teachers of that school, the Rivington and Blackrod example illustrating this well.

The idea of school-based in-service education as an 'opposite' of external patterns of study is capable of being interpreted as something having greater import than concern with physical location or accommodation. Thus it may be conceived of as work which though taking place on a school's premises, is planned by the staff of that school for the teachers' own professional advancement. It is in this sense that David Warwick[1] recommends it in his book, *School-Based In-Service Education*. A supporting argument is that within the learning community of the school's teachers and pupils, needs can be identified more easily, in-service experiences can be devised and related more closely to these needs, and resistance to implementation of teaching/learning outcomes of these experiences is likely to be less.

The limitations of school-based in-service education, especially if a school relies entirely on its own resources, may be equally severe as for externally based work. Members of staff drawing exclusively from their own resources may risk becoming over-insular in their attitudes and outlook, while individual teachers may be confirmed in existing prejudices. In any event, almost all the schools other than large comprehensives will be hindered by practical constraints in mounting in-service activities that could meet all staff requirements.

To avoid possible ambiguity of meaning, it is probably best not to refer to school-based in-service education at all, but instead to call any in-service work that is conducted on a school premises in response to the initiatives of the staff school-located, thus suggesting no more than topographical significance. This permits the work that is planned, initiated and controlled by teachers of the school, exemplified in greatest detail in the Ashmead report, to be described as school-directed. Moreover, any in-service education which relies on the expertise or experience of members of the school staff or which uses the accommodation, equipment or materials belonging to the school, can be understood as school-resourced. Clearly, when in-service activities take place on the school premises, they will be school-resourced and school-located; but when the school makes use of its teachers as tutors, equipment or materials for in-service work off the premises, as for example by Hartcliffe when organising a residential weekend, the in-service work will be school-resourced but not school-located.

This brings us to consider the central notion of school-focused in-service education, a notion which is in process of replacing the school-based approach as the stronger and more meaningful idea.

In the report[2] of a conference called to develop national and local policies for in-service education, school-focused work was described as the in-service education which is able to meet the identified needs of both the school and its teachers and to improve the quality of education for children at that school. What does this statement imply?

It can be argued that within the context of in-service education of its staff, 'the school' is not an entity that exists in its own right. Rather at any one time it comprises a large group of individuals – the pupils, and a second, small group of individuals – the teachers, every child and each adult possessing his own specific needs. Furthermore, it can be argued, every pupil's educational needs can only properly be met in school through exercise of the professional services of individual teachers, that is, on a one-to-one basis.

In a non-optical sense, to focus means to concentrate attention on something of interest or concern. Thus school-focused in-service education may be imagined as an activity which stems from concentrating attention on perceived professional needs of individual teachers serving in a school and through these teachers, the perceived educational needs of each of their pupils. School-focused in-service education can be designed and initiated specifically to meet these professional needs, but only indirectly children's educational needs.

Pauline Perry[3] defines school-focused in-service education as 'all the strategies employed by trainers and teachers in partnership to direct training programmes in such a way as to meet the identified needs of a school, and to raise the standards of teaching and learning in the classroom'. At first sight this definition appears to shift the emphasis of action from meeting the needs of individual teachers to the needs of the school. However, the apparent difference in emphasis becomes understandable when all professional needs, whether experienced on an individual basis, in functional groups or within membership of the total staff, are accepted as school needs.

The school-focused approach may be adapted and planned to meet minor or major innovation in the school embracing curriculum or organisation change. Thus a member of staff who wants to obtain help on marking English essays illustrates the likelihood that many of these perceived professional needs may be relatively small or short-term and easy to deal with. At the other extreme, planned change could affect the whole membership of a functional group, such as the pastoral care teachers at Hartcliffe, or the staff, for example at Benfield, examining the pros and cons of mixed ability teaching. It is therefore likely that since many planned changes will be responses to a school's new policies and will be reflected in its stated aims and objectives, school-focused in-service education may well have the additional important function of supporting staff development which was the declared purpose, of course, at Moons Moat. As all the teachers and, indirectly, the pupils are potentially the target of this in-service work, the focus can be construed as institutional in character.

In theory a school-focused programme of work could be planned and directed from outside the school (as appears to have been the experience of Norton Priory at Llandudno). But this could diminish the standing of the teachers of the school since control of the programme including key decision-making would reside elsewhere. For these and other practical reasons, it is preferable for such work to be school-directed. As the institutional requirements of the school determine reference points for staff development, the teachers should assume collective reponsibility for analysing professional needs (and through them the educational needs of the pupils), for deciding how and by whom these needs should be met, for activating the programme and ultimately for evaluating its effectiveness.

This raises the question: Should the school-focused programme directed by the staff be school-resourced and school-located?

Central to any commitment to school-focused in-service education is a tacit acceptance that direction of the programme operating from within the school should seek to utilise all relevant in-service resources irrespective of whether they belong to or are controlled by the school or some external body. Ideally, what matters in planning a programme is the appropriateness of the potential in-service study activity and the resources needed. Thus a school-focused programme is not to be understood as exclusively school-resourced and school-located. For instance, in meeting both the extension needs of the deputy head of a primary school and equivalent needs of other members of the staff, it might be decided to second him for a year to study for an advanced diploma in child psychology at a university. This resource would become available to his colleagues on his return, the external resource of the university having been converted into an internal resource in the person of the deputy head. Another example of a school's use of external resources is the Chesterton school-located course leading to an award-bearing qualification for which outside human resources were brought into school to provide the necessary tuition.

On reflection, it will be seen that the answer to the question in the last paragraph but one hinges on three crucial factors. These are:

(1) the purpose and scope of the programme;
(2) the size of the school; and
(3) financial/time constraints.

(1) *The Purpose and Scope of the Programme*

It was pointed out earlier that school-focused in-service education should be adapted and planned to meet innovation connected with curriculum and organisation development and would therefore have the important additional task of supporting staff development. Accordingly, the in-service programme should unfold in its purpose and scope in parallel with such staff development, in keeping with decisions determined by the head and his colleagues.

A modest in-service programme supporting minor change affecting members of staff might be school-resourced in its entirety, such as in a middle school where a teacher with advisory responsibility for mathematics could be asked to assist other teachers in strengthening their own teaching of the subject in the school. In contrast, a more ambitious programme endeavouring to support major staff development in the longer-term, for instance in helping to initiate an innovatory policy for reading in a primary school, might not be fully capable of realisation unless a tutor from a local college of higher education was brought in as consultant to lead a series of discussion sessions with the staff.

(2) *The Size of the School*

Other factors being equal, the larger a school and therefore the number of its staff, the greater will be the range and variety of resources available for sustaining a school-focused programme of in-service education. It is not difficult to speculate over what should be possible in a big comprehensive containing eighty-plus teachers compared with a small primary school having half a dozen members of staff. Yet the undoubted advantage of a large school in possessing many resources is likely to be counterbalanced by its teachers displaying a greater variety and number of professional needs. Nevertheless, however well endowed, the big school may not have resources for meeting all its needs. In two areas of professional work this is immediately evident: one involves the lack of certain specialists and specialist materials (for example, to whom can the subject specialist in a department of one turn in the school for specialist help?); the other involves the need to call in external evaluators periodically who could as experts bring a detached measure of objectivity to the assessment of certain in-service activities.

(3) *Financial/Time Constraints*

Money and time constitute two major limitations on a school-focused programme. Sending teachers on external programmes or courses, full- or part-time, is expensive whether these activities are poolable or non-poolable.

Also, visits to a school as part of its school-focused programme by outside tutors or consultants will be costly, not only because of the hidden expense of the salaries of the visitors but, additionally, because of travelling and/or maintenance expenses that may have to be paid.

Time constraints affect the release of teachers from school during working hours when salaries still have to be paid. Thus teachers may be required to be absent for three hours from the classroom – one hour's journeying in each direction to and from a teachers' centre ('wasted time') and one hour's participation on a course at the centre.

It goes almost without saying that in the interest of sustaining a strong school-focused programme, the school will want to obtain the best possible resources, calling on them from whichever quarter is judged most suitable, and applying them at locations convenient for the staff. But because of these practical constraints, the programme may have to be far more self-reliant than otherwise might be thought desirable. For this reason the Rivington and Blackrod experience has much to commend it.

There is one other aspect of a staff's own resources for school-focused work that should be considered and that is the programme's overall leadership. Since by general consensus the work ought to be school-directed, this implies that internal human resources at various levels of school management from the head down will be called upon to initiate and develop the programme, and frequently to tutor or lead discrete components of study.

The overall leadership of a school-focused programme constitutes the one task that ought not to be delegated to external parties. Senior members of staff, by virtue of their ascribed roles in the school management structure, are unable to evade responsibility for exercising leadership in this respect. The resources that these teachers represent are non-negotiable. It is therefore crucial to the outcome of planning that teachers holding key positions in school – and here we are thinking particularly of head, deputy head and head of faculty – do possess appropriate innovatory skills for curriculum and organisation development, and have a working knowledge of the potential contribution that might be made by outside providers. The programme's eventual success may rest on the quality of decision-making exercised from above, particularly in knowing when, from where and under what circumstances external resources can be used to reinforce the school's own contribution.

In the accompanying diagram (Figure 4.1) the various ways in which school-focused activities directed from within the school may be resourced and located are indicated by means of a simple analysis. Also, an example of a possible in-service activity is shown for each of the four combinations of resource and location.

SOME EXAMPLES OF SCHOOL-FOCUSED WORK

To give an indication of the kind of work that may be incorporated into a school's programme of in-service education, there are included below some examples of activities which, to a greater or lesser extent, use accommodation or other resources of various outside bodies:

The teaching practice resource centre of a college of education, containing many audio-visual aids and curriculum materials, is made available to serving teachers for the same two evenings a week throughout the summer term. It is attended regularly by three members of a school's subject department developing some project material for pupils.
A group of teachers from several middle schools making 'home-made' science apparatus in the workshop of a teachers' centre are invited to bring their products to one of these schools and demonstrate them to the staff.
A business studies teacher spends a day in another school where the subject is strong, to find out about a new Mode 3 CSE course.
One of the deputy heads in a large comprehensive school, responsible for students on teaching practice, spends a day at college with his opposite numbers from several other schools finding out how tutors organise students' allocation to schools.
The faculty of education in a polytechnic offers a short course on infant mathematics, lasting two evenings per week for five weeks. An infant school nominates two members of staff to attend this course and summarise their findings to the rest of the teachers on their return to school afterwards.

The humanities faculty of a secondary school invites a teacher from a neighbouring comprehensive school to assist in developing an integrated studies course for pupils in the fourth and fifth years.

The head of a large primary school that has successfully operated team teaching for several years is invited to talk to the staff of another primary school on how to introduce this kind of work and avoid pitfalls.

The teachers of a secondary school going comprehensive decide to run a two-day staff conference. They invite a lecturer from a university department of education to attend as an observer and evaluate the proceedings.

A full-time exchange is organised by a primary school and a college of higher education. This enables a tutor to teach for half a term in the school and for the deputy head to lecture students on aspects of initial teacher education at college during the same period.

An LEA adviser offers a school-located course of drama for juniors lasting for four successive Tuesday afternoons from 2.45 to 3.30 and involving practical work with children. After each session, the members of staff participating take part in half an hour's discussion with the adviser.

The staff of a comprehensive school ask the leader of a teachers' centre to organise a short course on their behalf at the centre. This course would have resource-based learning as its subject and involve outside speakers. Moreover, it would be held on three successive afternoons in the spring term from 2.00 to 4.00. In the event, it is run twice allowing different groups of teachers from the school to attend, their timetabled duties being temporarily reallocated.

Three small adjacent primary schools decide to pool their resources for in-service work. They invite a tutor on reading and language development to lead a series of six discussion sessions informally structured. These are school-located, taking each school in turn. All the teachers from the three schools attend each session. The work leads to a follow-up session at the tutor's college when the teachers are able to examine reading materials in the reading centre at their leisure.

Two department heads for the same subject in neighbouring comprehensive schools evaluate each other's work and the work of their departments over a period of a term, comparing notes afterwards.

A college of education as part of its service to schools offers weekend conference facilities including residential accommo-

School-focused in-service activities
can be

School-directed — — — *yes* — or — — — Externally-directed

Possible in theory
but undesirable
in practice. Thus
consideration of
resources and
location does
not arise.

Such activities can be:

School-resourced — — — — *yes* — — — — — — — — — — *yes* — — — — — *yes*
or
Externally-resourced
and
School-located — — — *yes* — — — — — — — — *yes* — — — — *yes* — — — — *yes*
or
Externally-located

and thus:

Totally self-sufficient	Partly self-sufficient	Partly self-sufficient	Non self-sufficient
e.g. a meeting of a group of teachers in school to examine a topic of mutual interest	e.g. a staff conference held at a local teachers' centre	e.g. a working group of teachers in school, with external consultant present by invitation	e.g. a teachers' workshop on micro-teaching held at college, led by tutor with CCTV

Figure 4.1 *School-Focused In-Service Activities: an Analysis of their Resources and Location*

dation in a hall of residence. Four primary schools in a nearby town choose a weekend to suit their preferences, and arrange a joint conference including the use of internal and external contributors towards the common theme.

An institute of higher education over a period of three years mounts school-located lectures comprising modules of an in-service B.Ed. programme at the request of teachers from the staff of the junior school.

The principal of a sixth form college and members of his senior management team invite an LEA adviser to help plan their 'college-focused' in-service programme.

A teacher of a post which is to become redundant owing to falling numbers is nominated by the school to undertake a one-year part-time conversion course (one-and-a-half days per week) at a nearby polytechnic. This will enable him to remain on the staff of the school though changing subjects.

Some Words of Caution

Though the school-focused approach to in-service education undoubtedly represents an advance in meeting teachers' needs in school compared with the more traditional methods, there are pitfalls and these should not be under-rated or ignored.

Probably the foremost is the danger of embarking on too ambitious a programme. Until the staff of a school has developed its own expertise in work of this kind, it would be sensible to plan on the basis of some narrowly cast professional needs as reportedly happened at Rivington and Blackrod. Many individual examples of school-focused work given above would make a suitable starting-point for a compact programme. Once the latter had been running for a term or two, its directors could raise their sights to widen the scope of the work. The programme could then aim to meet teachers' needs on several fronts at once or could be made to last for a greater period of time.

Another potential weakness is that the programme might be badly planned or carried out and this could negatively affect some members of staff who may already be dubious of the general benefits of in-service education. If such teachers were to attend sub-standard courses organised externally and at a distance from the school, the ensuing damage might be minimal. But if the teachers took part in in-service activities, specifically purporting to meet their teaching needs, which were inadequately organised by their immediate colleagues in school, then the practical outcome could be serious and the school-focused approach put at risk, at least for the immediate future.

The weight therefore that should be attached to planning, implementing and evaluating the school-focused programme cannot be overemphasised. The practical effects of these, which are discussed in some detail in the next three chapters, must be applied from within the school to ensure that the work as a whole moves forward smoothly and that as a result of review it can lead whenever possible to follow-up activities within a later cycle of an evolving programme.

NOTES AND REFERENCES: CHAPTER 4

1 Argued in D. Warwick (1975), *School-Based In-Service Education* (Edinburgh: Oliver & Boyd), ch. 1.
2 See H. Bradley (1978), *Towards a National and Local Policy for In-Service Training*, report of a national conference organised by ACSTT at Bournemouth, 17–19 January, p. 3.
3 Given by Pauline Perry in a keynote address to OECD/CERI International Workshop on School-Focused INSET, West Palm Beach, Florida, 6–9 November 1977.

Chapter 5

The School-Directed Programme: an Action Model

The basis of planning any change affecting the work of the school revolves around four main questions:

Where are you?
Where do you want to go?
How are you going to get there?
How will you know when you have got there?[1]

What seemes undeniable is that in-service education which is school-focused does not make a great deal of sense unless it is conceived of in relation to the suggestion of planned change implied in these questions and can be designed to support it.

Furthermore, there will frequently be occasions when the driving need will be to strengthen existing practices; the programme of work must be framed to assist in these directions too.

Besides distinguishing between some terms connected with change in school which are commonly used at the present time, this chapter proposes a general model or structure which can serve for implementing a school-directed programme attending to the school's needs, problems and requirements.

PLANNED CHANGE IN SCHOOL

Change in school – or for that matter anywhere – can be of two kinds, planned or intended and unplanned or unintended change. Of course sometimes unplanned change may be beneficial, for instance when a weak teacher holding a key post unexpectedly resigns and moves to another school. But more often than not, unplanned change is unhelpful since it tends to inject into the school feelings of uncertainty and indecision, and can be chaotic.

Planned change, with which we are mainly concerned, is in sharp contrast to this. It is an intentional alteration in the structure and functions of a school which may affect any of its educational intentions, processes, or products. Such change marks a departure from an existing situation or practice to a new or different one.

Planned change may be regarded as a generic term which includes innovation on the one hand and renovation or renewal on the other. Innovation is a process whereby ideas are generated, selected for further refinement and eventually adopted for use in the school. Renovation is not necessarily all that far removed from innovation, the difference being partly in the limited degree of change involved and partly in the retention or reapplication of existing intentions, processes or products.

In practice, pure innovation is rarely come across; and nearly all planned change in school includes varying degrees of innovation and renovation. Thus the introduction of a new subject, such as Chinese, into a school's sixth form curriculum might at first sight appear to be uncomplicated innovation. Actually, such an inception would probably involve adaptation and accommodation to policies and procedures already operating and would make use of the many teaching methods and strategies employed by teachers of other subjects, particularly those of French, German, or Russian, and so on. Where the need in school is to strengthen existing practices, for instance in teaching pre-reading activities to children in nursery schools or in reception classes of infant schools, the emphasis may almost completely focus on renovation with minimal change.

Support for the connection between innovation and renovation comes from Cyril Poster[2] who in his book on educational management in the secondary school, states that innovation may be considered desirable in order to *renew* the school's commitment to its ideology or overall educational aims. Thus in seeking to understand the meaning of planned change, any sharp distinction between innovation and renovation must be ruled out. The relationships between these kinds of educational change are summarised in Figure 5.1.

BRINGING ABOUT PLANNED CHANGE

In suggesting that planned change should centre on four questions, there might be added a rider. 'Who in the setting of the school would want to ask them?' It could be an individual teacher wishing to improve the effectiveness of his performance in the classroom or an *ad hoc* group of teachers acting concertedly to develop an integrated topic. It might even be the members of a department or faculty working to improve some aspect of pupil assessment, or the head and senior staff collaborating in seeking solutions to problems involving falling rolls.

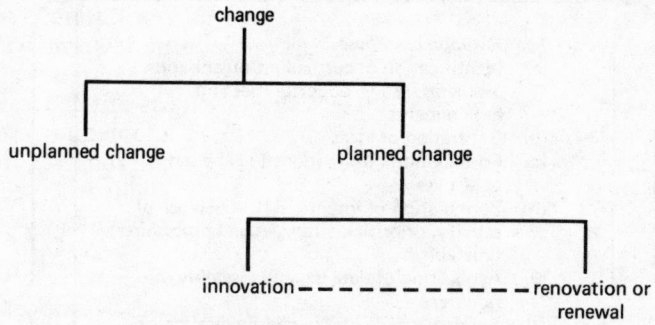

Figure 5.1 *Kinds of Change*

This is not to say that solutions to problems requiring change in school will come easily. It is common knowledge that schools are generally conservative, and for reasons which are often understandable there may be considerable resistance by teachers to change. Without wishing to be unfair to the profession, it is probably true that only a minority of teachers would want to accept an innovatory role. Most would claim their reliance on proven and well-tried methods. Thus we should not underrate the extent of resistance that there could be in trying to bring about planned change, however modest, in school.

The model in Figure 5.2 indicates how planned change may be effected in school by working successively through several phases and sub-phases. The model also shows that in-service education is available to provide support for this sequential process of planned change, as is educational research. Both, therefore, may be regarded as potential tools of the teacher.

Pared to essentials, it is possible to think of any single planned change – and there may be several such changes taking place in the school at any one time – as consisting of three distinct phases: a development phase, an implementation phase and a review phase. In order to picture the total process of planned change, it is perhaps useful to imagine each of these three phases (and their sub-phases) as self-contained entities. But clearly, intended change as shown in the model often does not occur in a neat sequence of chronological events. Take for instance a typical change which could affect a primary school. First one teacher and then a second might adopt new procedures for improving the presentation of pupils' written work. After a period of trial and error during which standards are seen to rise, the new procedures eventually become adopted by most teachers in the school.

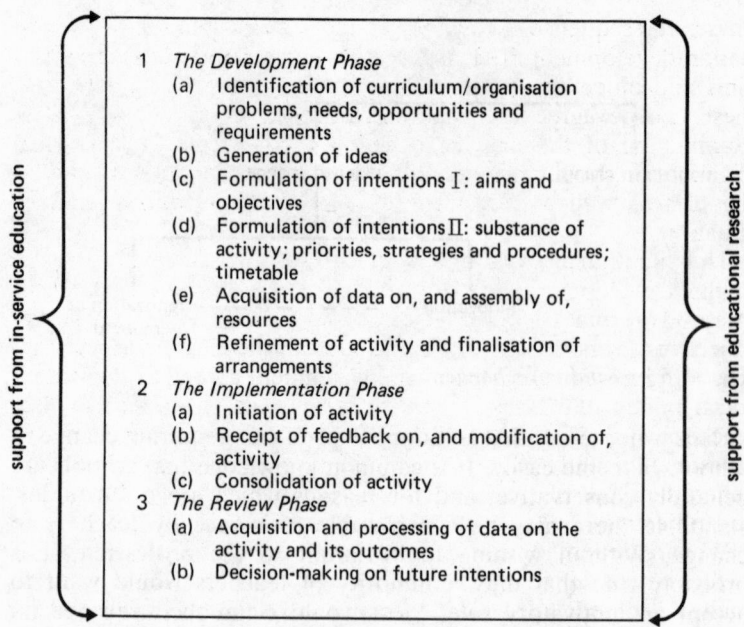

Figure 5.2 *Model of the Process of Planned Change in School*

Thus some phases or sub-phases of the sequence may be telescoped, have their order altered or even be missed out altogether. Given its practical limitations, the model enables the process of planned change to be seen as a whole and to be approached in a reasonably systematic manner.

(1) *The Development Phase*

Quite naturally, the staff of a school will be concerned with improving the school organisation and with improving better learning opportunities for their pupils so that these opportunities when put into practice in turn can bring about certain desirable changes in the pupils.[3] Thus planned change within the school which is school-directed and school-focused will tend to concentrate on curriculum problems and needs, and with matters inextricably tied to the curriculum such as timetabling, methods of assessment, staffing, external relationships, and so on. The development phase of planned change can therefore be seen to include what is generally acknowledged as curriculum development and organisation development.

Accordingly, the development phase will observe in its sub-

phases the sequence usually associated with curriculum or organisation development. The purpose of such a sequence is to select
aims and objectives ('Where do you want to go?'). But before
these can be agreed on, it is necessary to carry out a careful
examination of the existing situation ('Where are you?'). This
examination should include all the contributory factors, relating to
the past as well as the present, which have a bearing on the
situation.

This situation analysis, as it is known, will encompass all matters
in the Development Phase of the sequence (indicated by Sub-
Phases 1(a) and 1(b)) that precede the formulation of aims and
objectives (Sub-Phase 1(c)). It includes all the existing aspects of
school organisation and learning environment as well as the wider
social milieu of which the school forms part and in which the
teachers work. This analysis may therefore be interpreted as an
investigative study having a contextual reference which seeks to
generate and distil ideas, a prerequisite for formulating firm aims
and objectives.

We are indebted to Malcolm Skilbeck[4] for his assembly of
factors which define the change situation on which the situation
analysis is based. These factors are (a) internal and (b) external to
the school. The checklist affords a tool which teachers should find
useful in undertaking their own analysis. Adapted somewhat, it is
as follows:

(a) Internal factors
PUPILS
  abilities
  aptitudes
  interests
  perceptions
  personalities and temperaments
  socio-cultural backgrounds
  educational needs

TEACHERS
  abilities
  attitudes
  interests
  ideas
  values
  experiences
  knowledge
  skills
  education and qualifications
  special strengths and weaknesses

(b) External factors
DEPARTMENT OF EDUCATION AND
  SCIENCE
  legal requirements affecting
    teachers and schools
  policy statements and directives
    on education
  attitudes and advice of HMIs
  financial directives

LOCAL EDUCATION AUTHORITY OF
  SCHOOL
  teachers' conditions of service
  teachers' salaries
  policy statements and directives
  LEA attitudes, demands and
    pressures
  local political influences
  attitudes and support of advisers
  financial provision
  financial provision for schools

(*a*) *Internal factors* (cont.)

TEACHERS (cont.)
  roles within the school
  professional, academic and
    personal needs

SCHOOL ETHOS AND POLITICAL
    STRUCTURE
  history of school
  traditions
  common assumptions and
    expectations
  power distribution
  authority relationships
  methods of achieving conformity
    and dealing with deviance

EXISTING CURRICULUM AND
    ORGANISATION
  perceived and felt problems and
    short-comings
  anticipated needs and
    requirements

MATERIAL RESOURCES
  buildings and playing-fields
  room accommodation and
    allocation
  furnishings and equipment
  materials
  provision of ancillary staff
  allocation of capitation
    allowances
  potential for enhancement of
    material resources

(*b*) *External factors* (cont.)

SCHOOL GOVERNORS
  attitudes and interests of
    members towards life of school
  policies

OTHER EDUCATIONAL BODIES
  findings of educational research
  development of curriculum
    projects at national, regional or
    local level
  support systems of providing
    bodies for in-service work
  public examination requirements

LOCAL COMMUNITY
  cultural and social assumptions
    and expectations
  values
  political and religious
    considerations
  employment, non-employment
    and redundancy issues
  ethnic changes in neighbourhood
  attitudes towards pupils'
    behaviour

FAMILY
  parental assumptions and
    expectations
  attitudes towards homework
  changing relationships between
    adults and children
  social and cultural background

EMPLOYERS
  expectations and requirements in
    respect of literacy and
    numeracy, etc.
  technological change and its
    effect on curriculum needs

Once aims and objectives have been settled, decisions can be made over how implementation of the planned change can be carried out ('How are you going to get there?'). This may result in a statement outlining the substance or content of the change activity. It can also include sections dealing with priorities, strategies and procedures, and may include – at least tentatively – a timetable for action.

Subsequent sub-phases of development are concerned with acquiring *data* or information on possible resources, as well as actually assembling these resources in order to bring about the intended change activity. (Incidentally, much of the data referred to above may have already been obtained via the earlier situation analysis.)

Identifying resources for the proposed change activity may turn out in practice to be hard to do. Thus the final sub-phase of development will allow for refinement of the intended activity and for last-minute finalisation of arrangements.

(2) *The Implementation Phase*

However detailed and carefully executed may have been the planning during development, it is difficult to forecast in advance how implementation will turn out. We can be fairly certain that initiation of the change activity might result in unforeseen problems straightaway. These could range from relatively small things like pupils not getting to the proper room on time at the start of a new series of lessons, to more serious ones such as teachers not fully understanding their precise role in the change activity. A high degree of responsibility will therefore rest on the teachers directing the work to ensure that the lines of communication, verbal and written, are kept open. Colleagues and pupils should be encouraged to supply continuous feedback to organisers. This information will permit the new activity to be monitored, for deficiencies to be corrected and for essential modifications to be carried out while the work is proceeding.[5] Almost imperceptibly, the change activity will settle down into a period of consolidation when additional revision should become minimal.

(3) *The Review Phase*

It is logical to assume that when the change activity has run its full course, the teachers responsible for developing and implementing it will want to evaluate its success ('How will you know when you have got there?'). This phase will mainly be taken up with acquiring and processing data on the activity and the outcomes of that activity. It will almost certainly lead to a new round of decision-making, for instance on whether the activity should be rerun. These matters will be discussed more fully in a later chapter on evaluation.

IN-SERVICE EDUCATION IN SUPPORT OF PLANNED CHANGE

Given that any planned change which attends to the learning needs of the pupils or students, or to related matters involving classroom or school organisation, should form the major focus of attention for teachers, it is now possible to examine the central issue of how in-service education can be conceived of as a unified school-directed activity designed to resource, support and sustain this or any other relevant change.

Rapid reflection on the process of any particular change indicates that a teacher or group of teachers attempting to find solutions to a curriculum or organisation problem may easily experience specific professional needs. Furthermore, these needs may become apparent at any time during the sequence of this particular planned change. To give a concrete illustration: the teachers of a subject department in responding to the learning (that is, educational) needs of their pupils, might decide to introduce a version of team teaching in order to make the best use of the human and material resources of the department. Early on in the development phase of this planned change, the members of department might come to realise that they possessed little or no professional experience:

(1) in organising learning resources for pupils within a team teaching framework;
(2) of being able to teach as team members; and
(3) of knowing how to monitor the work output of individual pupils.

Later on in the review phase, some of the same teachers might feel that they were lacking in the skills for evaluating at the end of the school year the actual team teaching that had taken place. Here can be seen educational needs associated with planned change bringing into the open those related professional needs of the teachers. Such professional needs, which can be experienced at any phase or sub-phase of a sequence, are likely to be immediate since their realisation will be prerequisite to the performance of tasks being, or about to be, carried out in respect of the change activity.

The core of the argument is this: Teachers' professional needs arising from specific planned change can be met by planning and implementing equivalent in-service responses, the latter being complementary to this planned change. This supportive process is demonstrated in Figure 5.3 where Planned Change A leading to implementation of an appropriate change activity may generate certain professional needs A1, A2, A3, and so on. Each of these professional needs will invoke equivalent Planned Responses a1, a2, a3, and so on, which in turn will result in the implementa-

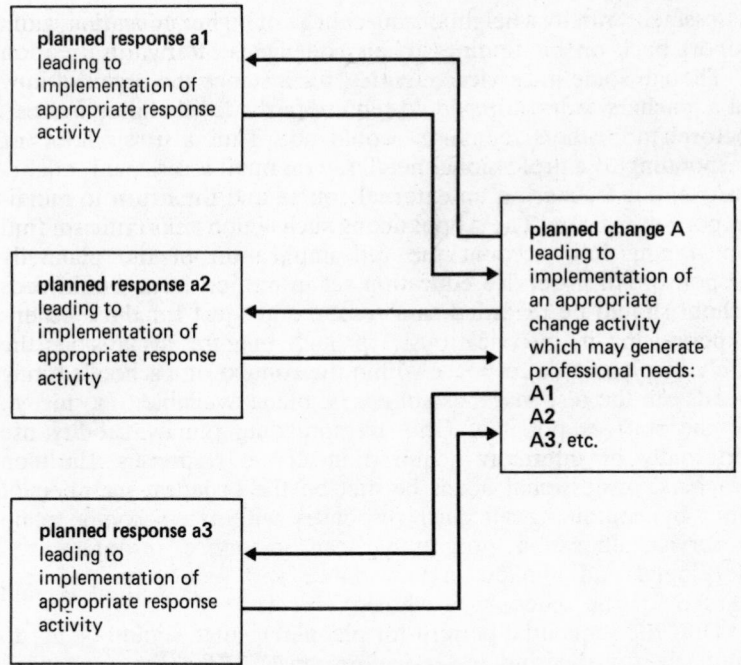

Figure 5.3 *Model Showing the Relationship of In-Service Responses to Professional Needs Arising from a Planned Change*

tion of respective in-service activities, more properly called response activities. When completed, these activities should help to reduce or satisfy the professional needs, thus enabling the original planned change to move forward to completion. The two-way arrows in Figure 5.3 indicate the need/response relationships between emerging professional needs and their corresponding in-service activities.

Using the examples of professional needs experienced in connection with team teaching, how can in-service responses be planned and implemented? Each response could of course take a difference direction. One response activity might be a teachers' workshop involving a series of informal meetings at which the department staff would hammer out solutions to the problems of organising learning resources. Another might consist of using an external consultant from another school who would from personal experience pass on team teaching expertise to the department staff; while a third response activity might require one of the department staff to attend a short external course on pupil assessment, run by a neighbouring college of higher education, and report back on his findings to his colleagues afterwards.

Though some in-service activities, for instance the organisation of a teachers' workshop, would require fairly detailed preparation beforehand, others seemingly would not. Thus a first school in responding to a professional need, say on pupil assessment, might just send a teacher on an external course and then turn to more important matters. The school taking such action risks criticism for not taking into account the full implication of the planned response. All in-service education set in motion from within the school should be regarded as a resource not just for the teacher experiencing it, but vicariously through him for his associates. Only by planning a response within the context of a school's total needs can the response's usefulness be made available to as many of the staff as possible. Only by spreading the availability of externally or internally acquired in-service responses can the teachers' professional needs be met on the broadest scale. And only by containing all such responses within a school's total in-service education programme can in-service resources be developed and applied in accordance with education policies agreed for the school as a whole.

Thus the sequential pattern for planned change should be used similarly for devising in-service responses. Like the sequence already described, the new sequence which consists of a parallel series of phases and sub-phases to those indicated in Figure 5.2 should be used as a procedural tool for in-service planners. As with the original sequence, frequently there may be occasions when some phases or sub-phases may have to be telescoped, changed in order or missed out. This new sequence is as follows:

(1) THE DEVELOPMENT PHASE
  (*a*) Identification of professional problems, needs, opportunities and requirements
  (*b*) Generation of ideas
  (*c*) Formulation of intentions I: aims and objectives
  (*d*) Formulation of intentions II: substance of response activity; priorities, strategies and procedures; timetable
  (*e*) Acquisition of data on, and assembly of, resources
  (*f*) Refinement of response activity and finalisation of arrangements.

(2) THE IMPLEMENTATION PHASE
  (*a*) Initiation of response activity
  (*b*) Receipt of feedback on, and modification of, response activity

(*c*) Consolidation of response activity.

(3) THE REVIEW PHASE
    (*a*) Acquisition and processing of data on response activity and its outcomes
    (*b*) Decision-making on future intentions.

The planned response's development phase: for meeting many professional needs, we can assume that development will be relatively straightforward to achieve. This is likely to be especially true when the school has to:

(1) respond to the clearly expressed professional need of a single member of staff;
(2) send a teacher or teachers on an external course; or
(3) organise a 'repeat' or second-cycle in-service response activity.

Development becomes harder when the teachers of the school plan a totally new in-service activity, especially if it is intended for several members of staff or if it is geared to professional needs imperfectly understood or imprecisely identified. Examples of when this type of development may be necessary include a staff conference on an educational theme, or a programme of action involving a series of visits to other schools for the purpose of obtaining information on open-plan learning. In planning for situations like these, the development phase will require careful and detailed treatment by the staff in their role of response-agents. Unlike the process of curriculum development, the development of school-focused in-service education is a concept about which little is known. Serving teachers, therefore, will have few precedents to guide them and consequently will have plenty of scope for working out new ideas to advance this form of development.

When responding to planned change, the ensuing in-service development will require a situation analysis. Like analysis of the original change situation, this new type of analysis will be concerned with examining all potential factors contained in Sub-Phases 1(a) and 1(b), that is, in development prior to formulation of in-service aims and objectives. This analysis, dealing with professional problems, needs, opportunities and requirements of teachers, will thus lead to the generation of suggestions and ideas, the precursors of explicitly accepted aims and objectives.

What factors will be included in the planned response situation analysis? Some but not all such factors will be those appearing in the checklist of factors for the planned change situation analysis.

But in the professional analysis, several groups of factors will assume greater importance than others. These are:

Internal Factors	External Factors
TEACHERS	DEPARTMENT OF EDUCATION AND
MATERIAL RESOURCES	SCIENCE
	THE LOCAL EDUCATION AUTHORITY
	OF SCHOOL
	OTHER EDUCATIONAL BODIES

Moving on to the implementation phase of the planned response, when external courses or other forms of in-service activity are selected by teachers of the school for use as the instrument of the response, the implementation's timing and pattern of organisation may come to depend on various factors beyond their control. Where such external direction of in-service work occurs, the outside providers fulfil the role of surrogate, that is, they can be seen to act instead of, and on behalf of, the staff. In contrast, when development leads towards in-service activities which are internal, that is, school-resourced, implementation will reflect a close measure of administrative control by the teachers and a time-scale which is likely to be more exactly adapted to the school's ongoing educational requirements.

And lastly the review phase: Whether an in-service response activity happens to be school-resourced or externally resourced, or whether this activity is passed to outside providers or retained by the teachers, it will serve as the product of a school-directed sequence of work and therefore automatically merit searching scrutiny from inside the school.

The School-Focused and School-Directed (SFSD) Programme
Implicit in this description of the process of planned change is the possibility that there will be several activities taking place in the school albeit at different phases of change and, moreover, over-lapping chronologically. To illustrate this state of affairs, we have shown three such changes in Figure 5.4 as Planned Changes A, B and C. There is also likely to be a variety of in-service planned responses devised to meet professional needs arising from these planned changes and they are indicated as Planned Responses a1 to a4, b1 to b2, and so on, on the left-hand side of the diagram. Collectively, they constitute the school-focused and school-directed (hence SFSD) programme.

Thus Planned Change A involving team teaching which invokes three in-service planned responses, in Cycle 1, is essentially the example we used previously. However, when a final review has been carried out, say at the end of the school year, thereby completing the cycle, a decision might be reached to 'repeat' the work in the following year, that is, as Cycle 2. Strictly speaking, the new work will not be a carbon-copy of the work in Cycle 1 for two reasons: one is that some alterations to the change activity (the team teaching) will be inevitable, and the other is that the development phase of Cycle 2 may be attenuated owing to work done and experience gained in Cycle 1 (the arrow pointing from Cycle 1 to Cycle 2 indicating this influence). Nevertheless, Cycle 2 might easily raise further professional needs in teachers, for instance needs arising from the introduction into the teaching team of an inexperienced teacher; and an instance of a response to these is indicated by Planned Response a4.

Planned Change B is included in the model of Figure 5.4 to illustrate the 'one-off' type of planned change involving a single cycle of work. For example, in a secondary school it might be decided to include photography in the list of fourth-year subject-options to be taught for one year only. In anticipation of this, a teacher is sent on a short course on photography at a nearby teachers' centre (Planned Response b1). On completing the course and returning to school, it is decided that he should pass on his new-found expertise to colleagues also likely to be involved in teaching the option (Planned Response b2). The arrow from Planned Response b1 to Planned Response b2 signifies that the latter depends to some extent on evaluation of the former, especially in its review phase. Moreover, it is likely that the situation analysis of Planned Response b2 will include some data deriving from Planned Response b1.

Using Planned Change C, we are able to demonstrate yet another set of in-service responses in the SFSD programme. Let us imagine that Planned Change C refers to the induction of newly qualified teachers into the work of the school (organisation development), an activity which is re-cycled year by year. Clearly, the experience gained in each completed cycle will influence what happens subsequently, and this effect is shown by the arrows pointing down from Cycle 1 to Cycle 2 and from Cycle 2 to Cycle 3. Corresponding to each of these three cycles, there will be one or more planned responses of in-service work for the probationers (shown as Planned Responses c1 to c4)). Hence in many schools a yearly induction education scheme will take place, indicated by Responses c1 to c3 respectively. However, evaluation of Planned Response c1 could affect the structure and content of Planned Response c2 and such influence is shown by a connecting arrow (as is the influence of Planned Response c2 on Planned Response c3).

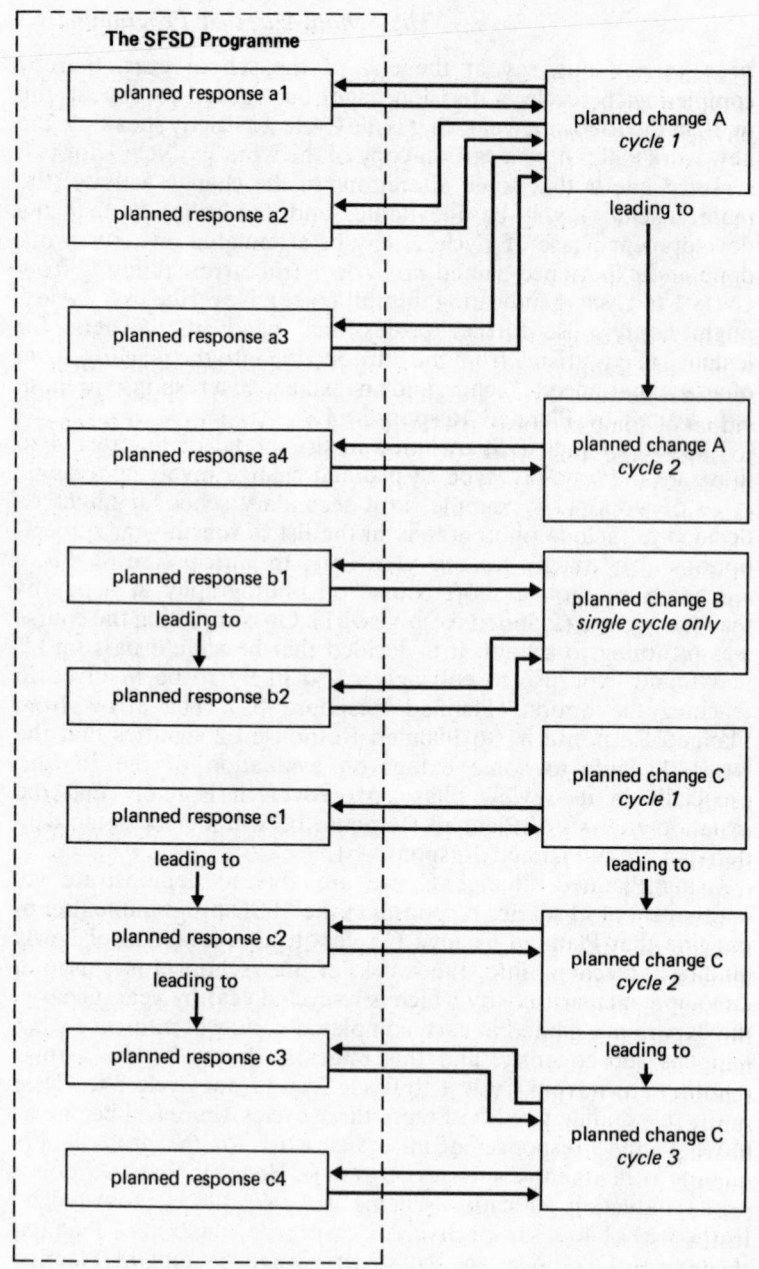

Figure 5.4 *Model of a School-Focused and School-Directed In-Service Education Programme in Support of a Number of Planned Changes in School*

Planned Response c4 is included to indicate an additional in-service activity arranged for one cycle of work only, for say a physics probationer.

In summary, the SFSD programme will be seen to:

(1) consist of one or more planned responses which may be at varying phases or sub-phases of completion; and
(2) have a starting date but is likely to be open-ended.

This leads us finally to ask whether it is possible to evaluate the whole programme and in particular to carry out some form of terminal review. Provided that a school has appointed an individual of some seniority on the staff (or a committee of teachers) to undertake this work, it is obviously desirable to keep the programme under continuous observation and to make any necessary modifications as it unfolds. Moreover, the SFSD programme may be assumed to run in notional cycles of one, two or more years in which case some form of terminal review can be effected at the end of each cycle, the results being assembled in a formal report for onward transmission to the school governors (as happened at Ashmead) or LEA, and so on.

EDUCATIONAL RESEARCH AND THE SCHOOL

Before ending this chapter, consideration perhaps should be given to the subject of educational research and its relationship with planned change in school, because in some ways it has a potential function which is suggestive of that of in-service education in respect of planned change.

Until very recently, educational research was widely thought of as esoteric, that is, a subject of interest only for those who were initiated into its mysteries. Researchers performed their rites and no one, least of all teachers in schools, was the wiser. Fortunately this state of affairs is now rapidly ending. For one thing, many more of the findings of educational research are relevant to schools than formerly. For another, the research methods presently being taught to teachers on advanced in-service award-bearing programmes are being taken into schools far more frequently than they were in the past. Thus educational research is ceasing to be a matter of little practical import to serving teachers. Instead, it can assist them in two ways – to facilitate planned change aiming to meet curriculum and organisation needs, and to illuminate planned responses designed to meet professional needs. Educational research is therefore to be seen as a practical tool available to teachers in charge of the work at any phase or sub-phase of a change sequence. Furthermore, as a tool it would be particularly effective in aiding development by gathering survey data, in helping to elucidate and solve problems, in processing data especially of the assessment type, and most of all in helping to evaluate all kinds of change procedures, imputs and outcomes.

Educational research is a resource which includes both knowledgeable individuals and the expertise at their command. Like other forms of resource, it may be located in the school (for example, in the person of a member of staff who recently might have completed a master's degree in curriculum studies) or outside the school (for example, via a university tutor who may be invited to evaluate some aspect of a change activity).

NOTES AND REFERENCES: CHAPTER 5

1 These familiar questions are asked by C. H. Barry and F. Tye (1975), in the last chapter, 'Innovation', of their book, *Running a School* (London: Temple Smith).
2 See C. Poster (1976), *School Decision-Making* (London: Heinemann Educational), ch. 8.
3 This statement is based on the definition of curriculum development given by A. and H. Nicholls (1978), at the beginning of their book *Developing a Curriculum: a Practical Guide* (London: Allen & Unwin).
4 See M. Skilbeck (1976), 'School-based curriculum development and teacher education policy', in R. Bolam (1976), *Teachers as Innovators* (Paris: OECD), pp. 81, 82.
5 Refer to Chapter 7 which deals with formative evaluation.

Chapter 6

Developing and Implementing the Programme

The aim of this chapter is to consider those policies that could be adopted by the head and staff for their own in-service education and how they could be arrived at.

It is true that many such policies, although acceptable in theory and technically in force in a school at any one time, may remain little more than mere intention unless clearly worked out procedures and strategies can be employed to give them bite. Even more than this, the matter of in-service priorities must be considered – and it is with this that the chapter ends.

THE SCHOOL'S IN-SERVICE POLICIES AND STRUCTURES

It is clearly the responsibility of the head and his colleagues to have policies operating that will cater for meeting the multiplicity of educational and other needs in the school and which will serve planned change. But it is only recently that this responsibility has been recognised as extending to include policies for the continuing professional development of the staff. But what does the term 'policy' convey? And what in-service policies could meet the staff's professional needs?

A policy is a general statement of intent indicating a broad field of action that should be taken or adopted in given circumstances. Sometimes, the statement describes a working rule rather than intent. A policy is normally concerned with realising major aims and objectives, and priorities. It may be explicit as in a written document or when teachers are informed at a meeting; alternatively, a policy may be implicit as a result of consistent action on the part of some or all of the teachers.

An example of the former method of invoking a policy might be when the head of a school, in a memorandum sent separately to each of his colleagues, indicated the kinds of in-service activity that would be suitable for inclusion in the SFSD programme; whereas implicit policy might be illustrated in the action of a deputy head who, over a period of time, consistently gave the same advice to teachers in charge of subjects as to how aims and objectives were to be constructed and presented in syllabuses, and so on.

Policies may be formulated at any level in the school organisation from the head downwards. It is quite mistaken to think that policy can only be made by senior members of staff. Thus at the highest level, the head might pronounce that all requests from colleagues for in-service resources from outside the school be channelled through, and negotiated via, him. But at lower levels such as that of faculty head, policies may have to be adopted that tie in with such a broader or definitive policy that is imposed from above. Thus a faculty head could require requests for external help made by his faculty colleagues to be discussed with him before being referred to the head. Such a lower-level policy is known as a derivative policy.

Some readers may need to be convinced as to why policies are really necessary in any complex organisation like that of a school. The explanation is that any given policy which has been in force for a period of time can be applied automatically in respect of a succession of situations which are broadly alike. Furthermore, a policy as a working rule is able to reduce strain and allow teachers to make decisions more quickly. Thus it may be school policy to refer all matters concerning in-service education to a professional tutor on the staff who has been specifically appointed, as at Heathland, to co-ordinate the work. Were such a policy not in force, teachers at a school might not know whom they had to approach each time they wanted to suggest or ask for some new in-service activity.

It would be inappropriate if not impossible to prescribe in-service policies that could be applied to all schools in every conceivable situation, nor would it be feasible to devise a prescription for a named school that could be held up as an example for others to follow. Nevertheless, what can be done is to pose some questions which teachers of any school might want to ask and which could lead to their making decisions on suitable in-service policies.

Are we prepared to commit ourselves to school-focused in-service education as a means of achieving staff development and, if so, what is the exact nature of this commitment?
What do we understand by school-focused in-service education?
What will be the aims and objectives of our programme of in-service study?
What practical limits shall we draw on the kinds of response activity that might be included in the programme?

What planning and co-ordinating machinery will we need, and when and how will this machinery be set up?

How will we identify problems and needs speedily, and with precision?

What procedures will we have to devise in order to ensure that policies are implemented smoothly and without undue delay?

What resources, human and material, will be available to sustain our programme?

What strategies will we have to adopt in order to achieve our programme's aims and objectives?

What guidelines will we need for establishing our order of priorities for the short- and longer-term?

What kinds of external resource will we require for our programme and how can we ensure that these are made available to the school?

What modes of evaluation will we need to build into our programme?

These issues touch almost every aspect of the curriculum and organisation of the school and it is therefore necessary to know who would be responsible for making major policy decisions on in-service education. Should it be entrusted to the headteacher? It is unlikely that school-focused and school-directed education will bring maximum returns to a school unless every teacher on the staff can be convinced that there will be something in it for him, that is, the work must demonstrate in advance that it will assist his career development in one way or another. Positive attitudes among teachers generally towards the benefits of in-service education, irrespective of whether it is school-focused, may not be generated unless as many members of a school staff as possible are given a stake in the policy-making processes. Paradoxically, in-service education is too important to be left exclusively to the head or a small number of teachers at the top of the school. How then may all the teachers comprising the staff be involved?

At this stage in our discussion it is necessary to introduce the concept of organic structure, for it is by selecting the most suitable structure within the organisation of the school that decision-making can effectively be carried out. Structure is taken to mean a framework in which individuals or groups of individuals, by virtue of their roles, are placed in relationship with one another. Committees, subject departments and house staffs come to mind as some of the more obvious examples of organic structures found in schools.

An argument which has much to commend it is that in every

school organic structures should be designed or, if they already exist, modified to facilitate planned change and to bring about corresponding planned in-service responses. Thus in every school there should be a supreme body charged with making definitive policies in respect of the curriculum, school organisation and in-service education of the staff. This body would be a democratic forum where the views of all the teachers could be heard and which would make policy decisions on behalf of everyone on the school staff. The argument can be extended to include similar structures established at lower levels too. Groups such as the teachers responsible for running a year could be charged with policy-making in which definitive policies received from above would be scrutinised and used to produce lower-level derivative policies.

In small schools – and these include nearly all primary and middle schools – the supreme policy-making body should be the whole teaching staff with the head acting as chairman. Not to be confused with ordinary staff meetings, policy-making sessions would be specially convened. These would enable the teachers as a whole to discuss educational and professional matters, and to frame their policy decisions accordingly.

In large schools, chiefly secondary, the practical difficulty connected with involving the whole staff (of up to possibly 100 teachers) in decision-making would call for a modified approach. Below are given two alternative structures which could be adopted as the school's supreme policy-making body:

THE REPRESENTATIVE COUNCIL
Senior staff from headteacher down to head of year, house or department would be *ex officio* members of this body, and the head would serve as its chairman. Other seats would be filled with teachers freely elected by the rest of the staff. Though representative of the whole staff, the Council could be susceptible to the criticism that it might take decisions from which non-members were able to dissociate themselves.

THE STAFF OPEN MEETING[1]
This structure sidesteps the problem of non-involvement by designating *some* but not all staff meetings for the purpose of policy-making. Chaired by the head (or his deputy), such meetings would be attended compulsorily by his senior colleagues. Other teachers on the staff who wished to take part in the proceedings would have the right to attend individual meetings. If they chose not to be present, their absence would

deprive them of being able to criticise decisions reached at staff open meetings. A variant of membership would be for 'non *ex officio*' teachers to be able to contract in voluntarily as full members for a fixed period of time (say one year) in which event their commitment to attend and participate could be regarded as binding. These two variants of involvement by a whole staff in policy-making at the highest level in the school may be seen as a collegial approach to management.

To understand how a representative council or staff open meeting could provide the machinery for policy-making, it is necessary to outline two contrasting types of meeting that are often confused, particularly in schools. These are the command meeting, frequently associated with decision-making in industrial, commercial and military undertakings, and the committee meeting, which is more commonly found in voluntary organisations. In Table 6.1 the characteristics of these two types of meeting have been assembled side by side in order to show their differences.

What often happens in school is that many meetings are held which tend to combine both types ineffectually. Depending on the level of importance (or nature) of the group, the headteacher/deputy head/head of department usually takes the chair *by virtue of his office* and the meeting – essentially a command meeting – is run on 'quasi-committee' lines *in order to give it a semblance of democratic legitimacy*. Decisions are arrived at by consensus after much talking ('wearing down the opposition') rather than by voting. Though such a meeting might have the appearance of a committee and yet in reality is command, in one important respect this arrangement cannot be avoided. This is because the most senior[2] teacher present will normally be held accountable to his superiors for any decisions which may be taken.

In the English educational system the headteacher and governors are legally responsible for all internal matters in the school. Thus collegial responsibility, in which the staff as a whole would share responsibility for all internal matters, is not possible as the law now stands. There is no choice but to accept that in the decision-making process it is the head who ultimately has to choose whether to accept or reject decisions provisionally made by his colleagues.

It follows that the command meeting is the type of structure that corresponds in practice with the majority of meetings that take place in school involving teachers. And of these meetings, the prime example is that of the ordinary staff meeting which normally is convened at the instigation of the head, is chaired by him and

Table 6.1 *Command and Committee Meetings: a Pattern of Contrast*

THE COMMAND MEETING	THE COMMITTEE MEETING
Meetings are called at the discretion of a convenor who serves in his role as externally appointed leader of the group.	Meetings are called at the discretion of the membership as a whole.
Each meeting is conducted by the convenor, acting as *ex officio* chairman.	Each meeting is conducted by a chairman who is freely elected by all the members.
Procedures and business are decided by the convenor, who may also determine the terms of reference.	Procedures and business are decided by all the members, frequently within terms of reference determined externally (that is, by a superior committee).
Actions taken, including decisions, are the responsibility of the convenor.	Actions taken, including decisions, are the responsibility of all the members.
All individuals must accept actions and decisions taken, even though they might not agree with them.	Individual members, whether present or not, must accept actions and decisions taken by the majority. If they do not accept them, they have the right to seek to get them reversed at a subsequent meeting or to resign their membership.
Attendance at meetings is compulsory.	Attendance at meetings is voluntary.
Functions of meetings are to enable the convenor to:	Functions of meetings are to enable the membership to:
(a) obtain information	(a) act in an advisory capacity
(b) test ideas	(b) co-ordinate activities
(c) give information	(c) act in an executive capacity.
(d) clear up misunderstandings	
(e) take action and make decisions	
(f) give instructions.	

conforms to rules of procedure selected by him. Unlike this, the committee meeting – called, for instance, to bring together a like-minded group of teachers voluntarily for the purpose of developing an integrated teaching topic – is relatively uncommon.

Thus to give members of a school staff maximum participation in policy-making as opposed to policy-implementation would require – legal considerations apart – modification of existing structures and a departure from normal working practices in school. It would demand a shift away from command-type meetings in the direction of committee-type and committee meetings. Hence many command-type meetings (such as the staff meeting, representative council, staff open meeting or department meeting), though continuing to be chaired by appropriate ascribed office-holders (from the head downwards), would have to be more democratic in function. Thus rules of procedure would be decided by members, and in keeping with these rules they would be able to ask for items to be included on business agendas. Decisions would be arrived at by majority vote expecially at times when consensus was not clear-cut. And only in exceptional circumstances would the chairman exercise his ultimate powers of suspending rules of procedure, terminating or unduly restricting discussion, or making personal decisions at meetings that were contrary to the wishes of most of the teachers present. Beyond this, encouragement would be given to the establishment of many more voluntary working parties in school in the form of true committees that could attend to solving educational and professional problems and in meeting in-service needs.

The implication underlying these hoped-for practices is easy to grasp: In the sensitive areas of curriculum and organisation development, and in-service education, many changes are only likely to become permanent when teachers are convinced of their effectiveness. Until newly acquired attitudes and opinions are 'internalised', these changes may quite easily remain stillborn. The order of the day for those holding senior positions in schools must therefore be 'Suggestion not imposition'. Where change is needed, it will be achieved more readily in a democratic atmosphere in which encouragement is given to voluntary involvement in policy-making throughout the school.

PROCEDURES AND STRATEGIES

Just as policies are broad-ranging aids to planning, so procedures are instruments designed to implement policies. For example, it might be agreed policy for all written communications between members of a school staff to be made using a standard memorandum form on which basic data (that is, name of sender, name of addressee, time and date of dispatch, and so on) are inserted; in addition, this particular procedure might stipulate the name or names of appropriate office-holders who are to receive copies for information.

A procedure, unlike a policy, is characterised by being specific in its effect as it lays down a sequence of acts which must be undertaken in order to realise a particular policy or group of related policies. Thus to ensure the greatest measure of co-ordination, procedures frequently encompass the work of one or two more departments or other functional groups. And in order to achieve standard outcomes, once procedures have been adopted they become mandatory, that is, binding on those groups of individuals charged with implementing policies. Furthermore, before any procedure is adopted, there should be adequate research and planning, otherwise the new procedure might turn out to be an unsatisfactory redefinition of the earlier procedure.

What procedures should be settled in school before planned change and any accompanying in-service responses can take place? Here is a list of topics which could properly be the subject of agreed procedures:

(1) *Methods of Communication*
    written and spoken methods
    distribution lists
    channels, internal and external to the school

(2) *Command and committee meetings*
    rules governing the conduct of business
    rules governing the filling of vacant seats
    rules governing the placing of items of agendas

(3) *Phases of development and implementation*
    arrangements for selecting and achieving deadlines
    methods of allocating individual responsibilities
    methods of allocating resources

(4) *Information*
    collection of appropriate data
    collation of appropriate data
    compilation and layout of documentation

(5) *Monitoring, evaluation and review*
    maintenance of security and confidentiality
    record-keeping
    interview methods

(6) *Follow-up work*
    translating in-service experiences into classroom practices
    debriefing arrangements

NB These six categories are not to be regarded as mutually exclusive in their effects. Any procedure which may be devised could quite easily embrace more than one of them.

It is one thing to select in-service policies and to adopt procedures for developing and implementing these policies; it is another matter to know when and under precisely what circumstances these policies and procedures can be put into force. This is where the application of suitable strategies enters the reckoning. Thus it may be school (or indeed LEA) policy that all heads of department should undertake a short course outside the school in running a subject department. Moreover, there may be accompanying procedures whereby individual teachers needing these courses can be identified and designated for attendance, taking into account the internal demands of the school and the availability of such courses, and so on. As will be anticipated, some department heads would require little convincing of the need to attend such a course, others more. If the head and his immediate colleagues are prudent, they will have a strategy of action which can deal effectively with the various attitudes held by teachers on the staff. Thus to encourage reluctant heads of department to attend external courses, a suitable strategy might have to be applied which comprised any of these tactics: (a) to counsel individuals intensively, possibly with the help of external consultants; (b) to provide additional resources for individuals who had attended courses; or (c) to make no working concessions to individuals who had not yet attended courses and who found themselves disadvantaged by lack of appropriate expertise in classroom or department office.

So what is a strategy? Sometimes described as the art of generalship, a strategy may be regarded as a means for dealing with the actual circumstances in which a policy and its accompanying procedure(s) can be realised. A strategy should be applied consistently over a period of time in respect of a number of similar situations, although the actual tactics used might vary from one occasion or situation to the next. In the context of in-service education in school, there are many potential strategies which could be invoked. Essentially, they have applicability in two main areas: first, to enable individual teachers, or groups of teachers working on a common project or centre of interest, to acquire appropriate in-service study experiences; and secondly, for the purpose of designating and assembling internal and external resources to support particular in-service study activities.

It is often contended that intentional changes involving human behaviour can be brought about by three well-known kinds of strategy:[3]

(1) Some individuals will only modify their behaviour when they are made to do so. In school where teachers are expected to conduct themselves at all times in a professional manner, it is often felt undesirable to have to instruct colleagues to act in a particular manner, and for this reason teachers in senior positions may be loth to give direct orders to subordinates. Nevertheless, there are occasions in the school's daily life when teachers, deriving status from the offices they hold and exercising legitimate responsibility, will employ power coercive strategies in order to bring about changes. These may result in telling colleagues or in sending them written instructions on what they must do.

(2) Another kind of strategy depends, not on giving orders, but on appealing to people's innate sense of reason. It is maintained that if individuals are presented with rational and logical arguments, they will make the necessary deductions and alter their behaviour accordingly. This strategy, the empirical rational, would appear to have considerable potential in influencing teachers positively. Since teachers will claim that they are members of a learned profession and are therefore capable of listening and responding to balanced arguments, clearly the use by strategists of research findings and other forms of reported educational knowledge or experience ought to figure prominently in reinforcing such empirical/rational arguments.

(3) In some other situations, intended change can only be effected by indirect means. Thus will the help of people possessing expertise in groups dynamics and human relationships, it is possible to encourage individuals – especially when belonging to functional groups in schools – to modify their personal attitudes and values, which in turn may influence them to make or accept changes in their professional work. Changes brought about by consultants[4] or other 'change-agents' who possess these behavioural skills are therefore said to be responsive to normative/re-educative strategies. In several respects, when compared with other kinds of strategy the normative/re-educative holds the greatest promise for dealing with professional inertia among school staff since it starts from

the position where individual teachers actually are in their thinking and feeling. It encourages them to look critically and analytically at themselves, to identify their own problems and needs and to seek their own remedies.

All these kinds of strategies – and others too – will have their usefulness when developing and implementing an SFSD programme for the school. But it is likely that only occasionally would any single one be used on its own. A combination of strategies – including even stick-and-carrot methods – might be needed to bring about lasting change.

If whole staffs and whole functional groups should be charged with deciding in-service policies, who would make decisions on procedures, and plan and initiate strategies?

A tempting solution would be to establish an in-service committee, modelled possibly on the pattern of the in-service training committee at Ashmead, which could exercise some degree of responsibility for the SFSD programme. Furthermore such a committee, with functions potentially affecting all the staff, would be chaired by the head or another very senior teacher at the school. But there are two stumbling blocks with a body of this sort, particularly if it is to be more than just a consultative or harmless discussion group where teachers can let off steam. The first is that development and implementation of in-service responses cannot be divorced from the development and implementation of associated planned changes. Thus an in-service committee would have the weakness of being responsible for only part of the school's total programme of professional and educational advancement, responsibility for the rest lying elsewhere. The second is that were a committee to have policy-implementing (that is, executive) powers conferred on it, it could be involved in taking actions on procedures and strategies that would be at variance with actions that, more correctly, should be enforced via the normal management structures of the school. Worse still, this conflict might be compounded if the majority of membership of an in-service committee were staff-elected.

What this really means is that the safest course would be not to have an in-service committee, but to rely on the existing structures in the school. These would certainly include the normal office-holders operating at various levels in the staff hierarchy who could bring their executive functions to bear on development and implementation of the SFSD programme. The devolution of responsibility and exercise of this responsibility right down the normal management structure undoubtedly would help to maintain a unified approach to planned change in the school.

IN-SERVICE PRIORITIES

Quite clearly it would not be feasible, owing to a variety of reasons that will be discussed later, to mount an SFSD programme that from the outset could meet all the conceivable professional needs of the staff's teachers. For one thing, adequate resources to support distinct elements of the programme might not be at hand; and for another, it might not be practicable to seek to realise every need as it is articulated. Thus any identification ('market research') of in-service priorities in a school must allow for constraints that will signal in advance their influence within and beyond the school.

Defined generally, priorities are matters having an antecedent or earlier claim to consideration. For instance, in planning a school's in-service programme decisions may have to be made over whether to support the release either of one teacher on a year's full-time secondment to undertake a diploma course on, say, curriculum studies, or of three teachers on a part-time short course dealing with, say, computer studies. Assuming that both alternatives are desirable for the educational well-being of the school, it may be necessary to decide which of the two is to be regarded as more important or to be effected first. As a general rule, therefore, priorities may be established:

(1) in order of importance, and
(2) in order of time.

But in-service priorities should never be determined in a vacuum, and there are a number of factors which should be brought into the reckoning. These include among others:

(1) specific in-service activities required for developing a planned change;
(2) specific in-service activities required for implementing a planned change;
(3) extent to which the proposed in-service activity could con-tribute towards the wider educational needs of the school;
(4) the ugency or degree of professional need of the individual teacher;
(5) the motivation of the individual teacher towards in-service education;

(6) the individual teacher's career profile, viz.:
total length of service,
relevant teaching experience,
existing qualifications, and so on;
(7) availability of finance; and
(8) availability of time.

By gathering all relevant data at the time of the situation analysis of each planned response, it should then be possible to make an informed decision over priorities. And in turn, adoption of in-service strategies in the school will depend on having determined these priorities correctly.

NOTES AND REFERENCES: CHAPTER 6

1 This type of meeting is attributed to Cyril Poster (1976), *School Decision-Making* (London: Heinemann Educational).
2 'Senior', that is, in respect of appointment, not in age or length of service.
3 These strategies were originally suggested by W. G. Bennis, K. D. Benne and R. Chin (1969), in their book *The Planning of Change* (London: Holt, Rinehart & Winston).
4 The subject of consultancy is dealt with in Chapter 8.

Chapter 7

Evaluating the Programme

In his recent book on evaluation in school, Marten Shipman[1] says that a teacher's right to autonomy in his work rests on a duty to evaluate. He adds that if teachers are to decide what to teach and how to teach it, there must be a system for evaluating how successfully they are achieving their aims.

Teachers' in-service education can no more be exempt from a general commitment to evaluate than from any other forms of educational work being undertaken in school or directed by the staff. The theme of this chapter is therefore to condense into a compact statement what is understood by evaluation today, and then to consider these basic questions about the SFSD programme:

Who should undertake evaluation?
What should be evaluated and why?
How should evaluation be conducted?

EVALUATION TODAY

Until well after the Second World War, on both sides of the Atlantic evaluation was equated with measurement. Relying on techniques and tests developed and refined by behavioural psychologists mainly for the purpose of estimating intelligence, educational measurement provided the one tool of evaluation then available to LEAs, colleges and schools. In in-service education, such assessment as there was concentrated on the measurement of factual knowledge and improving skills. Examinations in their many different modes thus became predominant in assessing teacher performance. The main weakness tended to be that although it became possible to compare the performance of one teacher with another by examination, it did not allow meaningful or relevant comment to be made about the quality of such in-service study. For instance, did a particular course strongly motivate teachers who were participating? Was it taught in the best way by tutors? Were the examinations used on the course the most suitable way of assessing teachers' performance? And above all, did this in-service experience lead to better teaching when individuals returned to their classrooms?

A commonly accepted position now is that evaluation is chiefly concerned with making judgements. But judgements about what? In in-service education these will certainly include assessing the performance of teachers on programmes and courses, award-bearing or not. However, there are likely to be judgements about many other issues, some of which can be claimed to be more important than performance on courses. Here are some matters involving in-service education on which judgements may be called for:

The suitability of agreed policies and procedures.
The quality of leadership in planning and implementing the programme.
The appropriateness of the stated aims and objectives.
The effectiveness of planning decisions.
The numbers of teachers taking part in a programme.
The quality of teaching on courses.
The variety and availability of physical resources.
Methods of disseminating information.
The calibre of leadership of a programme.
The timing of particular study sessions.

But sound judgements can never be arrived at when there is a dearth of information. At best they will be sketchy, at worst downright deceptive. They must therefore be informed, that is, made to rely on evidence obtained beforehand. Such evidence must be accumulated through making observations either first-hand or second-hand, through reports of other onlookers or listeners, given by word of mouth or in writing. This information may be quantitative or qualitative in kind. In the ten instances suggested above, in given circumstances virtually every one could generate information of both kinds, the exact mix between the two varying in accordance with the precise requirement of each evaluation. Qualitative evidence tends to be descriptive, compara-tive and accrued in respect of individually characterised activities, for example by means of case studies. In contrast, quantitative evidence, for instance involving the length of study sessions or the number of teachers on particular courses, requires measurement, enumeration or statistical analysis in one form or another. Since data obtained in this way generally is easier to assemble and report on than qualitative data, most judgements will tend to be drawn from evidence predominantly quantitative. In summary, therefore, evaluation may be interpreted today as judgement deriving from evidence obtained mainly by measurement but also by description.

WHO SHOULD UNDERTAKE EVALUATION?

If one may be forgiven for misquoting Lincoln's definition of democracy, school-focused and school-directed in-service education can be described as 'education of the teachers by the teachers for the teachers'. What this implies is that evaluation of the SFSD programme ought for three very good reasons to rest primarily with the teachers themselves.

One is that in-service education of the teachers points to their being the customers or clients. Correspondingly, their perceptions from the receiving end in lecture or discussion room are likely to condition their attitudes towards the value of the tuition to which they are exposed and, ultimately, to affect their motivation towards in-service study generally. A second reason is that the school staff will normally be responsible for planning and implementing the SFSD programme. Although, as has been pointed out earlier, resources may have to be brought in from outside the school to fill gaps, provision – certainly in terms of centralised control – will chiefly be undertaken by the teachers. Inevitably and rightly so, evaluation of the programme will be an important aspect of this provision, while the final reason is that the programme will be designed and run for the teachers in order to meet their professional needs. It can be argued that the teachers are the best judges of the content or substance of an in-service programme provided on their behalf, and thus they ought to make it their business to evaluate what they are being taught

It is true that some aspects of evaluation, if not conducted by the teachers of a school, could be entrusted to parties outside. These might be LEA administrators, teachers from other schools, college lecturers, teachers' centre wardens or even 'lay' individuals such as school governors, local counsellors or parents.

For the teachers controlling the SFSD programme, it would appear perfectly proper to obtain the services of such external individuals who may be able to offer a greater degree of objectivity and independent thought than might be provided from within the school. Suppose, for instance, opinion on a staff was split over the potential benefit which could result from a planned series of discussion sessions dealing with new techniques of pupil assessment. It might be considered wiser to invite an outside evaluator to provide a report on the activity than for one or more members of staff to carry out the evaluation, members who rightly or wrongly might be suspected by their colleagues of prejudice or bias. In so far as any external report when handed over to those commissioning it would be read and given consideration (that is, evaluated) by its readers, it indicates that even when external assistance is provided, final evaluation must rest with the teachers themselves. As with Harry S. Truman, 'The buck stops here', evaluation of the SFSD programme must be the ultimate responsibility of its teachers.

WHAT SHOULD BE EVALUATED AND WHY?

To marksmen, targets can normally be seen from a distance enabling shooting to be concentrated in an appropriate direction taking into account wind-drift, the trajectory, and so on. Likewise the task of educational evaluators becomes practicable when they have been able to identify their targets and have adopted suitable means for reaching them. Thus within the context of in-service responses in school, evaluation targets will be located throughout all sequences of development and implementation. To conceive of any response without well-defined aims and objectives or suitable strategies and procedures would clearly be unthinkable, any more than it would be possible to make it without determining in advance the likely involvement of teachers taking part in the response activity as tutors or students. Thus it will be necessary for evaluation to be directed towards a great many aspects of a response.

Figure 7.1 shows the total range of possible evaluation targets in one planned response of the SFSD programme. It will be seen that two kinds of evaluation are indicated, summative evaluation and formative evaluation. And as will be explained, there is a big difference between them.

Suppose the teachers of a primary school have just taken part in a whole-day staff conference on, say, 'Traditional versus modern methods of teaching mathematics'. Strolling out afterwards, one teacher might say to another, 'I didn't get much out of that'; while the second replies, 'Oh, I don't know – the session after coffee-time was quite useful'. The following morning the head might call in the deputy head and several other senior colleagues for a short meeting to obtain their considered opinions. After due reflection on what they have said, he informs the whole staff several days later on how conclusions reached at the conference will be followed up in the future through the development of new policies for teaching mathematics in the school.

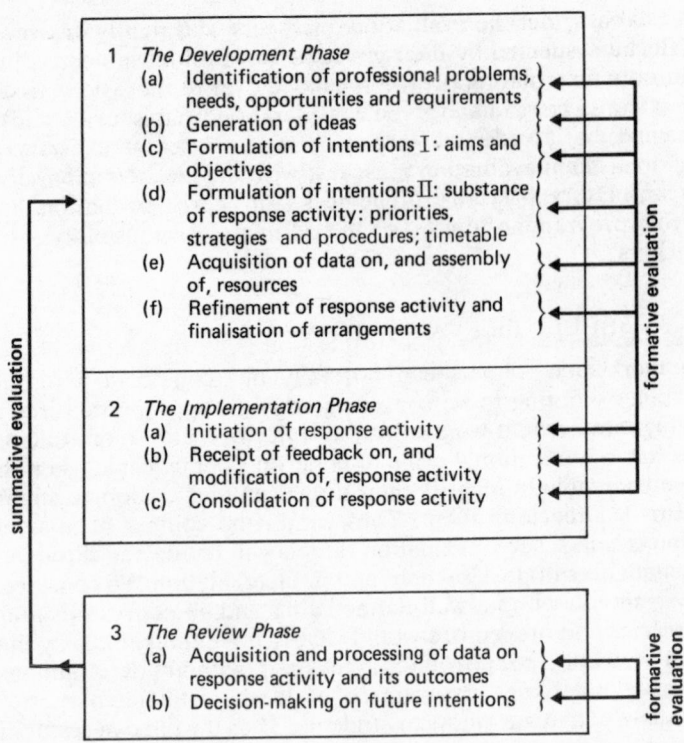

1 *The Development Phase*
  (a) Identification of professional problems, needs, opportunities and requirements
  (b) Generation of ideas
  (c) Formulation of intentions I: aims and objectives
  (d) Formulation of intentions II: substance of response activity: priorities, strategies and procedures; timetable
  (e) Acquisition of data on, and assembly of, resources
  (f) Refinement of response activity and finalisation of arrangements

2 *The Implementation Phase*
  (a) Initiation of response activity
  (b) Receipt of feedback on, and modification of, response activity
  (c) Consolidation of response activity

3 *The Review Phase*
  (a) Acquisition and processing of data on response activity and its outcomes
  (b) Decision-making on future intentions

summative evaluation

formative evaluation

formative evaluation

Figure 7.1 *An In-Service Planned Response: Targets of Evaluation*

This illustration has all the ingredients to show how the review phase of a planned in-service response can work. First, it shows that evaluation may be both informal – as when teachers chat among themselves – and formal – as when meetings are called to assess progress. And secondly, it shows that evaluation can take place immediately after termination of implementation, or be delayed until some time later.

This post-implementation evaluation is known as summative evaluation[2] and is applicable to all aspects of development and implementation (as indicated by the arrow on the left-hand side of the diagram). If the first two phases of the planned response comprise the whole target, self-evidently the stated aims and objectives represent the bulls-eye of that target. Any outcome of the work, successful or otherwise,[3] almost certainly will be evaluated in terms of whether these aims and objectives have been attained. In other words, this type of evaluation may be used to establish the overall effectiveness of a planned response.

Because summative evaluation has a consecutive position and can only take place subsequent to implementation, it is only able to affect decision-making in respect of future activities. Let us imagine that a middle school teachers' discussion group on gifted children has just completed a series of meetings. Here are some decisions that would be influenced by subsequent evaluation of such work:

Should the cycle of work be ended forthwith?
Or should it be allowed to take place again?
If the answer to the second question is in the affirmative, are minor or major changes necessary?

Evaluation leading to decision-making of this kind will undoubtedly be of interest to all members of the school staff who are involved whether as customers or providers (or both).

In the other type of evaluation, formative evaluation,[4] every aspect of each sub-phase in development and implementation of a planned response is a potential target. Formative evaluation serves as continuous feedback during unfolding of the whole sequence of a planned response. It is thus applied concurrently, not consecutively as with summative evaluation. Its purpose is to influence the shaping and working out of the planned response and it assists successive and continuous revisions which may be considered desirable throughout the development and implementation phases. Especially, deficiencies can be identified and corrected. One of its features is that formative evaluation can provide a monitoring function, the purpose of which is to strengthen and improve performance while events are happening. It has particular use for those teachers who direct the whole SFSD programme or who lead individual response activities. But it can also help those teachers being taught in that it can sharpen their perceptions, make them generally more critical and increase consumer feedback.

The nine reports of schools undertaking in-service work are, of course, summative with a heavy emphasis on the descriptive rather than the analytical or judgemental. Moreover, there is some evidence of internal summative evaluation in these schools in the preparation and issuing of reports for staff (Thomas Calton) or governors (Ashmead) or in verbal reporting back (Benfield). Formative evaluation, though not referred to as such, is implied in the task of co-ordination (Thomas Calton), in the work of the deputy training head and in-service training committee (Ashmead) and in that of the professional tutor (Heathland). However, one is left to conclude that formative and summative evaluation was very rudimentary in these schools and that if they were typical of most schools, far more needed to be done to improve evaluation procedures generally.

The function of formative evaluation in respect of Phase 1 and 2 of a planned response is now explained in greater detail:

(1) *The Development Phase — Sub-Phases (a), (b) and (c)*

In Chapter 5 it was stated that the main requirement at the outset of development was to analyse as completely as possible the response situation by reference to all the relevant factors. The process of evaluation should thus be extended to include the analysis while it is being carried out. This evaluation should have these general characteristics:[5] it ought to be exploratory, that is, designed to focus lines of inquiry that may lead in more directions than the obvious ones; descriptive, that is, made to apply to situations using less common as well as more common data and vocabulary; and comparative, that is, intended to examine actual situations in relation to intended situations.

Here are examples of questions to which evaluators could well want answers:

(a) *'Identification of professional problems, needs, opportunities and requirements'*

Are the problems exposed necessarily significant ones?
Are the problems accurately described, with conclusions properly drawn?
Have all the relevant needs been identified?
Has any attempt been made to put these needs in rank order of importance?
To what extent do these problems and needs compare with those identified in neighbouring schools?
Do these needs derive from, and relate logically to, identified problems?
Are the suggested opportunities for in-service education likely to provide motivational spin-off in other directions?
Have previous in-service experiences of teachers in other schools been taken into account?
To what extent have policies of the LEA been considered when suggesting possible in-service activities?
Has the summative evaluation of previous cycles of similar work been employed at this sub-phase of the planning?
Has a preliminary investigation been carried out on resources that might be required for the suggested response activity?

(*b*) *'Generation of ideas'*

Have all members of staff who wish to contribute towards development been given full opportunity for putting forward suggestions on aspects of the possible planned response?

Do the ideas which have been expressed follow on logically from the response analysis?

Are the ideas accurately presented in the ensuing documentation?

Have any insights into development of the planned response been overlooked?

(*c*) *'Formulation of intentions I: aims and objectives'*

Are the aims and objectives couched in simple, explicit and unambiguous prose?

Are the objectives expressed in suitable behavioural terms (that is, so changes in behaviour on the part of teachers as students can be observed or measured at the end of the in-service planned response)?

Do the stated aims and objectives reflect accurately the planners' ideas?

(*d*) *'Formulation of intentions II: substance of response activity; priorities, strategies and procedures; timetable'*

Have all types of suitable response activity been considered?

Has proper consideration been given to an order of priorities?

Have any priorities been overlooked?

Have the strategies for implementation been explained to all members of staff likely to be involved in the work as tutors or students?

What evidence is there that the strategies and procedures which have been adopted draw on the experience of running similar types of work elsewhere, or previously?

Do distribution lists for action or information contain the names of all people who will be involved or should know?

Does the plan of action permit adequate time for all aspects of development to occur?

And arising from this, are the deadlines realistic?

Have any crucial factors for the successful outcome of the work been accidentally omitted from the planning?

(1) (cont.) *The Development Phase — Sub-Phases (e) and (f)*
Until these sub-phases are reached in the sequence, the emphasis in development must be to determine aims and objectives and to agree how they may be realised. In these later sub-phases,

planning becomes translated into action since decisions now have to be put into practice. What effect will this have on the character of formative evaluation? The latter will continue to be comparative, though now happenings will tend to be looked at in the light of previously accepted intentions. But it will also be differential and critical in the sense that it will strive to show when or where data and resources may be inadequate for the projected in-service tasks or when or where the proposed in-service activity and its timetable are liable to be found wanting.

Here are some typical questions to which evaluators would want answers:

(e) *'Acquisition of data on, and assembly of, resources'*

Are the teachers in charge of development sufficiently knowledgeable of in-service programmes and courses offered by colleges to make decisions on where or when to send colleagues if the need arises?

Have the teachers compiled an inventory of individuals who could help with consultancy work?

Does the documentation clearly show how and when specific resources will be used in support of the planned response?

Are the arguments convincing on why some specific resources have been selected to meet particular needs rather than others?

(f) *'Refinement of response activity and finalisation of arrangements'*

Has sufficient time been allowed for throughout the projected timetable to allow specific objectives to be attained?

Are the intended study activities suitable for meeting appropriate objectives?

Are the study components correctly sequenced in the response activity timetable?

Does the starting date of the response activity need altering?

Does the final draft of the published timetable of the response activity require further, last-minute, amendment?

(2)   *The Implementation Phase — All Sub-Phases*

Moving to the response activity in operation, what should characterise its formative evaluation? Since the work will now be unfolding in accordance with decisions already made and will be keeping (or not keeping) to a timetable, the main task of evaluation will be not to make judgements on what might happen after the work has been completed but to provide continuous and immediate feedback on what is happening now. This is so that defects can be pinpointed and put right, and minor improvements made. It is during this phase that the general monitoring function of formative evaluation can be seen taking place in its most ready form. Thus evaluation throughout the phase of implementation should concentrate on those crucial aspects of the work on which success of the whole enterprise depends (for example, performance of tutors) in order to build an accurate picture of what is taking place. Moreover, evaluators should be encouraged to indicate possible remedies and alterations for the better. Summing up, evaluation of this phase is descriptive, specific, critical and suggestive.

These questions illustrate the approach of formative evaluation to the sub-phases of implementation:

(a) *'Initiation of response activity'*
Why were the arrangements for the opening session mismanaged, and what needs to be changed?
Why were there not enough sets of conference papers available for distribution to the school staff at Session 3?
Who was responsible for failing to brief the visiting speaker on the precise needs of his audience?
Why was a technician not detailed to supply an overhead projector?

(b) *'Receipt of feedback on, and modification of, response activity'*
Are the course tutors making the best use of feedback from evaluators?
And are they making the best use of feedback obtained informally from teachers undertaking the study?
What firm evidence is there that practical arrangements are being modified where they have been shown to be faulty?

(c) *'Consolidation of response activity'*
Have amended conference papers, substituted for the faulty originals, now been issued to participants?
Are course leaders or tutors keeping up-to-date records on the work as a whole?
Are these records sufficiently comprehensive?
Have arrangements been made to debrief teachers attending external in-service activities on their return to school?
What evidence is there that the response activity is now running smoothly and defects eliminated?

In practice the distinction between formative and summative

evaluation is not sharp. Thus formative evaluation undertaken during the time-spans of Phases 1 and 2 may quite easily provide a foundation on which summative evaluation in Phase 3 can be based. Indeed, some of the formative data and judgements may actually be included in the review report of Phase 3. Moreover, the report would undoubtedly be a factor which a Cycle 2 situation analysis could take into account.

Reference to Figure 7.1 shows that there is one further set of targets for formative evaluation to which allusion has not yet been made. These involve a special kind of formative evaluation whereby the terminal review of a planned response may be exposed to the attention of evaluators – an 'evaluation of evaluation' so to speak. The need for evaluation of this kind stems from a necessity to strengthen the procedures and methods used for determining the outcomes of a response activity and for informing a new cycle of decision-making. Typical questions that could be asked are:

(3) *The Review Phase — Both Sub-Phases*

(*a*) *'Acquisition and processing of data on response activity and its outcomes'*
Have appropriate questions been asked in order to identify the 'hidden curriculum' of the response activity?
Has evaluation data been obtained from all potential and relevant sources?
Will the review report be ready for distribution on time?
Is the review report written in simple English?

(*b*) *'Decision-making on future intentions'*
Does the review report contain clear-cut recommendations as to future action?
Were the summative evaluators able to do their job properly?

HOW SHOULD EVALUATION BE CONDUCTED?

To evaluate effectively, it is necessary to be familiar with the techniques that are available. The description which follows is concerned with outlining these techniques of evaluation and to indicate when any single technique is particularly applicable in the total evaluation process. The techniques applicable to formative evaluation are not in every case the same as those which can be used in summative evaluation, and in this description the distinction will be made.

What techniques are appropriate to formative evaluation? For reasons connected with costs and time, only exceptionally is it likely that an external 'professional' evaluator from university or college would be invited to carry out the work. Rather, the teachers of the school would expect to be responsible for evaluating development and implementation of a planned response themselves. The tendency therefore would be to use techniques that are unsophisticated and which could be applied, as often as not, informally.

In order to evaluate (by accumulating information and making judgements), there are four rules that should be applied in successive order:

Collect the information
Organise the information
Analyse and judge the results
Report the results and the conclusions.

Taking these in turn, how can this information be collected? It is generally recognised that there are three methods available to evaluators. The first is to ask people questions, the second consists of observing human behaviour (including acting as a silent witness of people talking and taking part in discussion), while the third involves examining documents.

Here are several techniques open to teacher-evaluators for collecting information:

(1) *Interviews*

At one extreme, questions can be asked in the form of the totally unstructured interview in which the evaluator follows his inclinations. In the middle is the interview where a set of previously prepared open-ended questions are asked. At the other extreme, the interviewer asks a set of closed-ended questions (that is, involving choice from a pre-determined series of responses). Such interviews can be carried out by those leading or tutoring in-service activities, by teachers attending sessions as students, or by third-party evaluators (for example, other teachers in the school).

(2) *Questionnaires*

People of course can be asked questions, not face-to-face but through the medium of a written schedule or questionnaire. As with the interview, it can include questions that are open-ended or closed-ended, or be a mixture of both types. Unlike the interview, however, the questionnaire must always be structured since the questions have to be prepared beforehand. Since the evaluator can subsequently extract information from completed questionnaires, they may be taken to serve as a form of documentary evidence.

(3) *Visual and Audible Observation*
With this technique, the evaluator will normally have to decide in advance what he wishes to observe in order to obtain appropriate information. To maintain consistency, these intended observations are normally itemised in a previously prepared checklist. The information required may be quantitative, for instance when the evaluator might wish to count attendances, or qualitative, for example in estimating the general interest aroused in a topic being currently discussed in some in-service sessions. Furthermore, his observations may be of two kinds: of people talking or taking part in discussions among themselves, or of people performing tasks, for example perfecting PE skills.

(4) *Keeping Records and Diaries*
These are really additional forms of making observations. They differ in that they do not usually rely on a compilation of checklists as *an aide-mémoire* to the work. Instead they rely on the quality of notes made during the observations while the latter are occurring. The advantage of keeping records and diaries is that untoward or unique events can be noted down, allowing unanticipated conclusions or judgements to be made afterwards.

(5) *Obtaining Information from Existing Documents*
There is much information that can be gleaned from a whole host of documents of varied kinds – from literature advertising or giving details of future courses or activities external or internal to the school; from review reports containing summative evaluation of earlier response activities; from course handouts, booklists, and so on; and from memoranda or other forms of correspondence between tutors, leaders and students. All such documents have potential use to evaluators.

These five techniques can also be used for summative evaluation. But there is another, sixth, technique which is applicable because of its character to summative evaluation only. This is pre- and post-testing which is designed to find out whether behavioural objectives have been met. For instance, to check whether teachers have acquired particular skills, they can be given tests before embarking on an in-service activity, and be given identical tests afterwards. A variation of this technique is to give participants who took part in a response activity a questionnaire to fill in containing questions about their classroom practices – for example, it might be designed to established which ideas or teaching strategies outlined in the response activity on, say, biology were used with the students' pupils beforehand and which of these they intended to use in future.

What about organising the information for evaluation purposes? A great deal of it is numerical and may therefore lend itself to being dealt with statistically. Much data obtained through interviews, questionnaires or by direct observation should be tallied on previously prepared sheets divided into columns, rows, and so on. However, other information such as that recorded in a diary or log-book cannot conveniently be treated in this way. Hence the evaluator may have to apply another procedure in order to assemble his material. To help him in his ultimate task of making judgements, he will need to isolate facts or ideas that may be significant. Thus they might be typical of particular phenomena or modes of thinking, or they might be unique. As a result, the evaluator can assemble a collection of relevant data for further processing.

This brings us to consideration of how these findings may be analysed and judged. The information, having been condensed or assembled into suitable numerical or qualitative-type form, will now be ready for scrutiny. Thus raw aggregates of statistical data may be converted into percentages, proportions or ratios permitting comparisons to be made. Also, some aggregates may be placed in rank order to display popularity of choice or frequency of response. Other simple calculations available to the evaluator include the reckoning of averages, medians (that is, half-way frequencies or values) and modes (that it, most popular frequencies or values). In turn, these statistical results enable the evaluator to make further comparisons, and draw conclusions including making judgements. Moreover, he might then be in a position when he could make suggestions or recommendations for future action.

Qualitative data of course cannot be analysed like this. The evaluator should always remember the danger of generalising from a particular case. He is on safer ground if he can direct his analysis towards interpreting relationships (such as cause-and-effect) and links, or in making comparisons and contrasts between individual items of data. His conclusions, when arrived at, should be tentative, moderate and cautious.

And lastly, how can the results and conclusions be reported? The answer hinges very largely on the use intended for the evaluation. By the very nature of formative evaluation which is designed to influence and improve outcomes, much of the work of evaluation is likely to be undertaken informally. Hence much of the reporting of formative evaluation is also likely to be informal, that is, disseminated in the form of comment by word of mouth or via memoranda circulated between colleagues in school. But there may be occasions when formal, written and more detailed statements are called for, especially on summative evaluation. For the most part, the latter should be structured under these headings: 'The purpose of the evaluation'; 'The findings'; 'The conclusions'. 'More detailed' does not mean that written reports should be voluminous. On the contrary they should be characterised by their accuracy, brevity and clarity.

NOTES AND REFERENCES: CHAPTER 7

1 See M. Shipman (1979), *In-School Evaluation* (London: Heinemann), introduction, pp. ix–xi.
2 The terms 'formative evaluation' and 'summative evaluation' were coined by M. Scriven (1967), 'The methodology of evaluation', in R. W. Tyler *et al.*, *Perspectives of Curriculum Evaluation*, AERA Monograph on Curriculum Evaluation No. 1 (Chicago: Rand McNally), pp. 39–83.
3 'Outcomes' are often described as the product of a change or response activity. Hence the term 'product evaluation', used by some writers, which is virtually synonymous with summative evaluation.
4 See note 2 above.
5 This characterisation of formative evaluation is based upon the well-known work of D. L. Stufflebeam *et al.* (1971), *Educational Evaluation and Decision Making* (Itasca, Ill.: Peacock). He identifies four kinds of educational decisions for evaluation to serve: planning, programming, implementation and recycling decisions.

Chapter 8

Resourcing the Programme

It is clear that in-service work, whether related to the needs of teachers in particular schools or not, will only make headway if appropriate and adequate resources are allocated. Well before a school's in-service SFSD programme is launched, in the planning stages it will be necessary to establish what resources can be drawn upon and to decide when or where to deploy them.

The chapter is concerned with three issues: first, identification of the range of potential resources internal and external to the school; secondly, consultancy; and thirdly, the constraints that may mitigate against using these resources to their best advantage.

POTENTIAL RESOURCES

The identity of all potential resources for every activity of the SFSD programme should be made known early on during planning. This process of identification should be given high priority in the development phase of an in-service response to planned change. As part of the situation analysis, resource identification should be undertaken in some detail in order to obtain as full a picture as possible of how teachers' professional needs may be met. Resources for the programme may be identified internally or externally, although in practice various constraints – some of them severe – may limit their effectiveness in meeting these needs. These potential resources may be typified under these seven headings which will be examined in turn:

(1) human resources
(2) accommodation
(3) equipment and materials
(4) library resources
(5) 'packaged' in-service activities
(6) financial resources
(7) teachers' working time.

(1) *Human Resources*

The chief human resource – and one that has been least regarded and most under-utilised until very recently – is the school's own staff. This statement can be backed with some firm supporting evidence. The recent DES survey[1] found that between 60 and 70 per cent of all teachers in regular service undertook in-service study of one kind or another, a surprisingly high proportion. This by any standard represents a wealth of largely untapped and newly acquired expertise that should be made available to colleagues in teachers' own and neighbouring schools.

Parallel to the gaining of in-service knowledge is accumulation of working experience by teachers in previous as well as present schools. But how often do schools prepare and maintain systematic records of previous teaching experiences and courses attended by members of staff that would be of help in a school's SFSD programme? Not often, one would imagine. Of the nine schools reported on, there was little evidence that internal staff resources were being used other than for heads of department to counsel probationers and for the professional tutor to advise heads of department (Heathland). And yet to tap such resources would seem to be an essential outcome of a detailed response analysis.

Apart from the teachers of a school, there are many different people who have a potential contribution to make to the work from outside. They include teachers in nearby schools, advisers, HMIs, Schools Council field officers,[2] teachers' centre wardens, and lecturers from colleges and universities, all working in different branches of the education service. They could help in a whole variety of ways. Outsiders with expertise might be invited in accordance with the school's in-service requirements to early discussion or planning meetings, as well as be asked to take part in or lead sessions connected with response activities.

In addition, there are experts from a number of other professional backgrounds who also have links with schools and who would, if invited by the teachers, come and talk with the staff or lead sessions of study. These include parents working in industrial concerns in the vicinity, school governors with particular knowledge of local government and members of the health and social services, to name but a few.

Clearly, there are many precedents for schools' use of outside speakers, not least for giving talks to pupils. It is thus not surprising that most of the nine schools are on record as having invited external tutors for help in their in-service work. This was most evident in the tutorial support provided by Homerton College to Chesterton School in the award-bearing course, while

Hartcliffe's involvement of the National Marriage Guidance Council illustrates the use of expertise from outside the teaching profession.

(2) *Accommodation*

As with other types of resource, a school would be well advised to look discerningly at its accommodation and to decide what could be used for in-service work. Does the school have a comfortable staffroom that, if need be, can seat all the teachers for meetings? Is there a suitably sized hall for showing films, giving demonstrations or mounting exhibitions of materials? Discounting ordinary class-rooms, are there enough rooms which can be used for small group discussions? What laboratories, workshops, craftrooms, and so on, are available for developing new teaching skills?

It is hardly necessary to be reminded that school premises are not always the most convenient, comfortable or professionally motivating places to undertake in-service study, particularly if teachers are expected to attend voluntarily and in their own time, such as at weekends. An investigation of possible in-service venues may therefore require looking at accommodation in neighbouring schools, teachers' centres or colleges, and even buildings belonging to non-educational organisations such as a conference centre, industrial premises, public library or hostel.

In periods of financial stringency, few if any school staffs can afford to reside, as did Norton Priory, for two-and-a-half days at a leading hotel. But a half-day or whole-day session at a local college (for example, Chesterton) seems a more realistic proposition.

(3) *Equipment and Materials*

It would be an advantage if the school were to compile a brief *inventory* of equipment and materials that could be included in its SFSD programme. This inventory could include details of hardware, software and apparatus of special or noteworthy interest. On balance, one would imagine that a purpose-built school should possess more modern and up-to-date equipment, and so on, for in-service work than other schools. But this view might be contradicted by the presence in less well endowed schools of home-made apparatus (for example, for science) or audio-visual aids (for example, for history or geography) designed and used by teacher-enthusiasts. In any event, inventories containing such information should be made available (possibly with the help of publicity given by LEA advisers or teachers' centre wardens) to neighbouring schools so that they too might make use of the facilities for their programmes.

Nearly all LEAs have assembled collections of curriculum (and other) materials in resource centres or teachers' centres,[3] and information is normally disseminated to schools on the identity of these materials and how they can be borrowed by teachers. Only recently have providing institutions, except in respect of library facilities, come to recognise that they have a responsibility within their capability to assist schools by loaning resources. Few colleges, as yet, issue inventories of equipment or materials which they are prepared to lend to teachers. In the absence of information, schools would be advised to take initiatives in contacting institutions when they have specific requirements. There is little doubt that most colleges would be willing to reciprocate.

One or two colleges in sparsely populated areas such as North Wales have invested in caravan trailers which are adapted to house appropriate educational equipment and materials (for example, for teaching reading) and to provide room for in-service study. Thus it is already possible for some schools, particularly small rural schools, to call on mobile accommodation of this kind. Clearly there are many other resources, as yet unrecognised and untapped, that await the ingenuity of SFSD programme planners.

(4) *Library Resources*
Some schools habitually collect books, pamphlets, magazines and journals for the use of the teachers, such as at Moons Moat, these being placed in the school library or held by the deputy head or professional tutor. But there are further documentary resources that the school can identify or collect. Thus it might become standard practice for teachers attending external courses or other in-service activities outside the school to submit a report (not more than, say, one side of handwritten A4) which could be placed on permanent reference for colleagues. Similarly, teachers leading or tutoring elements of the SFSD programme might be required to submit brief review reports which could also be made available to colleagues. At least two of the nine schools (Thomas Calton and Heathland) are reported to have requested such written reports. Thus it is clear that schools engaging in in-service education have been taking this aspect of their work seriously.

Looking beyond the school, there are many excellent library facilities in university departments and institutes of education, polytechnics and colleges. Nearly all of these are willing to loan books, sometimes in small batches, to serving teachers in nearby schools. Even travelling libraries belonging to LEAs should not be overlooked as a possible source of educational and professional literature for in-service work.

What other means are there for providing in-service information to teachers? One involves an imaginative use of an in-service notice-board located in the staffroom or other prominent place, on which can be displayed all relevant data. Another is to make effective use of the staff bulletin (when such an 'in-house' publication exists). Distributed individually to all members of staff, it can serve to give details of impending in-service functions or to provide feedback in condensed form of in-service functions which have been recently attended by colleagues.

(5) *'Packaged' In-Service Activities*
Included under this heading are all programmes and courses which are offered by external providing bodies on a formal basis. Stress is laid on the importance of having someone on the staff of the school who, as head, deputy head or teacher-tutor with overall responsibility for the day-to-day running of the SFSD programme, can develop links with lecturers in outside institutions which mount these 'packaged' activities and can acquire a good working knowledge of available courses, and so on. It is no coincidence that Chesterton's award-bearing course was set up largely at the instigation of the deputy head who had been a member of the college staff and who presumably knew the ropes. These school–college links are needed so that teachers may be effectively counselled over in-service possibilities and opportunities outside the school. As a rule, external institutions are keen to strengthen relationships with schools. They will as a rule be pleased to accept invitations and overtures from schools to meet teachers with responsibilities for developing in-service activities.

(6) *Financial Resources*
In times when money is scarce, it is essential to make the most effective use of funding which is available to schools. When LEAs provide assistance to teachers attending external in-service activities, financial help may range from 100 per cent reimbursement of all expenses (normally payable for courses attended at the employing authority's behest) to reimbursement for some of the travelling expenses only (made for attendance at courses of 'fringe' usefulness). Courses and other in-service activities organised by employing authority advisers or teachers' centres are normally offered free (that is, are equivalent to 100 per cent grant for attendance); while often reimbursement for travelling expenses is based on two rates, one for in-county journeys involving a straight mileage allowance and another for out-of-county journeys which is based on the appropriate bus and/or second class return rail fare.

Schools do not have any direct control over funds disbursed in these various ways. Normally such money is allocated in keeping with LEA policies, administrative officers at county halls having some discretion in the manner by which individual teachers may be granted financial help. Heads are sometimes able to make special cases on behalf of deserving colleagues and thereby influence the disbursement of money to a limited extent.

What funding might be directly available to a school for developing and implementing its own in-service work? The purchase of educational books, magazines, journals, and so on, should present no difficulty, though orders placed for this literature may reduce the amount of money available for children's textbooks. Few LEAs as yet include funding in school budgets specifically for teachers' in-service work. However, in appropriate circumstances money raised voluntarily, for example through a school's parent–teachers' association, might be channelled in this direction.

(7) *Teachers' Working Time*

A review of possible resources would be incomplete without referring to one kind that can easily be overlooked. This is teachers' preparation or non-teaching time in school hours which is usually used for marking or administrative purposes. With worsening pupil–teacher ratios, this margin of time, particularly in small schools, is in short supply, and more often than not gets eroded because of absence due to illness, and so on. Clearly, if any of this preparation time can be made available for in-service work, it would have to be allotted without prejudice to other more pressing needs of the school and its teachers.

CONSULTANCY AND THE SCHOOL[4]

For some time it has been evident that there are in the teaching profession many people – serving in a variety of establishments and possessing different career backgrounds – who command expertise, experience or knowledge that would be of considerable benefit if it could be channelled towards a wider educational audience. This consideration is specially relevant at those times when the cost of generating new resources for teachers' in-service education becomes acutely more difficult.

There are of course a number of serious practical problems to be overcome before use of such human resources can be common-place: In what *form* would the resources represented by know-ledgeable and experienced individuals be acceptable to serving teachers? How could we identify these people? How could they and teachers in particular schools wanting their services be put in touch with each other? The notion of consultancy has been developed recently in order to try to answer these and other important questions.

Though not everyone is happy with the use of the term 'consultancy' to describe the intended type of relationship between the practitioner in school and the individual with expertise, that is, the consultant, nevertheless there is general acceptance that responsibility to seek professional help or information (that is, to decide to consult) should rest with the person requiring assistance. It is the teacher in classroom or school who in the first place should take the initiative. Significantly, by deciding when or in what circumstances he would wish to call on the services of a consultant, he is able to retain his freedom of action, a hallmark of the truly professional person.

This notion of consultancy is hedged about with question-marks because it is not immediately apparent when an individual with expertise should be approached. Ought he to be invited at the very outset to discuss with the teacher a problem or need perceived imprecisely at this early stage? Or should the consultant come in after the problem or need has been defined?

Broadly speaking, there are two possible ways of responding. If the consultant is brought in at the beginning his role is basically clinical. Since nothing of substance in terms of problems, needs, goals or remedies may have been worked out by the school, he can help to define the situation as part of the ongoing process of change. His role, like that of a psychotherapist, is one of guidance and analysis rather than of imposing remedies. His function is to help the teachers identify their problems, to voice their needs, to frame their goals and to decide on their remedies. Thus the consultant will not be there to offer expertise in the form of knowledge, but as someone who understands human relationships and the dynamics of organisational change. This approach is called process consultancy as it is concerned with means rather than ends. And sometimes the analogy of the chemical catalyst is employed to describe the function of the process consultant.

The second way of responding to requests for help is after the teacher – with or without the assistance of process consultancy – has provisionally articulated his needs. Thus he might want help in developing a syllabus of work or in organising team teaching within his department. It is at this stage that a person possessing expertise in a particular subject or area of work may be called in.

Acting jointly, the consultant and teacher can then tackle the specific task in order to solve the problem. Of necessity the role of consultant is a subtle and balanced one. For as Ray Bolam[5] has pointed out: 'If the consultant adopts a directive or prescriptive stance ... he ceases to be a consultant and becomes a trainer or conveyor'. The relationship between consultant and teacher requiring mutual respect must therefore be collaborative at all times and lead, through continuing dialogue and combined enterprise, to the realisation of concrete objectives. The contribution of the consultant complements that of the teacher, the former's expertise being matched by the latter's knowledge and understanding of the particular circumstances of his school and pupils. Because of its purpose which is to achieve tangible end-products, this type of consultancy is known as task consultancy. The role of engineer or technicist is probably the closest we can get in describing the function of the task consultant.

We have not yet made it clear *who* should be consultants. There is no doubt that the overriding principle is that, other things being equal, the best man or woman should be encouraged to undertake the work irrespective of existing position or background. Thus a consultant could teach in the same school as colleagues wanting help (internal consultancy) or be based in a neighbouring school, teachers' centre, college or university (external consultancy).

In some schools already, teachers can be identified who have a consultancy function written into their contracts of employment. We may quote two examples to illustrate this. In one the professional tutor in a comprehensive school (for example, Heathland) might be expected to fulfil on behalf of his colleagues the type of activity which has been called process consultancy. And in another, a teacher – sometimes designated teacher-consultant for a particular subject, say mathematics – might be appointed in a middle or primary school to provide task consultancy to the staff on all matters pertaining to the teaching of his subject.

External consultancy is in its infancy and, almost certainly, will remain so for some time not least because of the difficulty of relating supply to demand. Requests for assistance from teachers in schools are likely to be uneven. It is not hard to see that this could place considerable strain on those providing institutions and LEAs which have been starting consultancy services. How one institution (Bristol Polytechnic) in association with its parent LEA (Avon) and three other LEAs comprising a sub-region in the south-west have attempted to meet this challenge is briefly described by Sefton Davies[6] in a timely article. It gives an inkling of the issues to be resolved before external consultancy can be offered to schools on a regular basis.

This brings us, finally, to consider who should be responsible for identifying external consultants and for putting schools in touch with these people. Undoubtedly, it is the LEAs and their advisory staffs that have a crucial role to perform in connection with these matters. Since the tasks of maintaining schools, employing teachers and ensuring educational standards must come within the remit of LEAs, it is right and proper that, largely by means of their advisers, they should monitor and oversee consultancy work as part of their total in-service provision for teachers.

Wardens of teachers' centres might also have a potential role to play, not least in publicising and disseminating information on external consultants to all schools in their geographical areas. But also, because of their neutral position, wardens may well be able to contribute towards process consultancy.

PROGRAMME CONSTRAINTS

A necessary aspect of planning the SFSD programme should be to make allowance for any constraints or limiting factors that might reduce or in some other manner interfere with its effectiveness. These constraints are largely connected with resources.

Like other forms of education, any programme of in-service education for teachers is bound to be labour-intensive, that is, it has to rely heavily on tutorial expertise for its operation and success. The financial cost of this tuition can be met either directly, by charging individual teachers fees for courses they attend, or indirectly by billing their schools or debiting the cost to the teacher's or school's LEA. Whichever of these procedures is adopted, expenditure on tuition will be relatively more than on alternative forms of possible in-service provision such as 'distance learning' (via the mass media of communication or correspondence courses, and so on) or by making library or audio-visual aids resources available to teachers from centrally held collections belonging to LEAs.

Moreover, labour-intensive activities are more expensive to provide than those which are materials-intensive. In-service programmes, therefore, are likely to be demanding in respect of students' fees, tutors' salaries and the travelling and maintenance expenses of both tutors and students. *Costs* of all kinds will be without doubt a major drain on the development and operation of the SFSD programme. Linked to this, the location of external resources in distant or inconveniently sited colleges or teachers' centres, and so on, must be seen as another factor limiting overall expenditure. For these reasons, it seems to be clear that strategies should be employed for implementing a programme which utilise the school's own resources as much as possible. For a school to achieve a high degree of self-sufficiency in its own in-service provision is a goal which will be in keeping with general sentiments to trim or anchor costs.

Another major constraint involves teachers' conditions of service. In England and Wales, salaries are settled at the national level by the Burnham Committee, while conditions of service are decided within the framework of the Schools Regulations[7] by LEAs individually, after consultation with each other and the teachers' unions. The latter have always been hesitant in negotiations to concede any increase in working hours which would enable compulsory in-service work to take place at the end of the school day immediately after the pupils have gone home, or during vacations. This unwillingness of unions has also been due to the fact that since salaries and conditions of service are negotiated separately, it has not been possible to trade concessions in respect of in-service education in exchange for additional remuneration on behalf of teachers.

Except then for the twenty half-day sessions that may be deducted from the standard 400 working sessions of the school year (allowed for under the Schools Regulations) which governors of all schools are permitted to designate as occasional holidays and which can be used in certain circumstances for in-service study, there is little time during working hours when teachers can be expected to take part in in-service work at school or elsewhere. In short, study that is programmed to take place in out-of-school hours has to be conducted on a voluntary basis.

If or when changes in the negotiating machinery at a national level are made, they may then permit teachers' salaries and conditions of service to be worked out jointly. In exchange for an improvement in salaries and a more generous reimbursement of expenses incurred by teachers on courses, it might be possible for substantial periods of time to be allotted for mandatory in-service education.

Until such time as the conditions of service are altered on these lines and, moreover, substantial funding becomes available, the SFSD programme will tend to be restricted to the school's own premises and be held in normal working hours or immediately afterwards, and only infrequently on other occasions.

NOTES AND REFERENCES: CHAPTER 8

1   See Department of Education and Science (1978), 'Induction and in-service training of teachers: 1978 survey, *Statistical Bulletin*, issue 8/78, December 1978.

2 A list of current field officers is available from the Schools Council (see Directory of Resources, section D on Schools Council).

3 A list of teachers' centres with collections of curriculum materials is available from the Schools Council (see also Directory of Resources, section D on Schools Council).

4 This section of Chapter 8 substantially appeared as an article by the author in the journal *Teacher's Time*, vol. 10, no. 3 (Nov./Dec. 1979), pp. 3–5.

5 See R. Bolam (1976), 'The types of environment most likely to favour the active and effective participation of teachers in educational innovation', *Teachers as Innovators* (Paris: OECD), 1, pp. 8–69.

6 See R. W. Sefton Davies (1979), 'The role of the providers', *British Journal of In-Service Education*, vol. 5, no. 2, pp. 8–10.

7 The full reference is the *Schools Regulations, 1959*, SI 1959, no. 364, dated 5 March.

Directory of Resources

Information that will be of help to teachers developing in-service programmes in their own schools.

A JOURNALS

A small number of British journals regularly and frequently carry articles having special interest for those involved in organising in-service work in or out of school. These are described below:

British Journal of In-Service Education

Published three times a year on behalf of the National Association of Teachers in Further and Higher Education (NATFHE), the journal is the only academic publication that deals with teachers' in-service education. The annual subscription is £7.50 (post free) payable to Mr J. G. Lee, College of Ripon and York St John, Ripon, N. Yorkshire HG4 2QX.

Teacher's Time

This journal is currently published nine times per year by Messrs Eye to Eye Publications Ltd, 107–11 Fleet Street, London EC4, from whom it may be obtained. The annual subscription is £4 (post free). Besides providing articles on and giving details of programmes of study, leisure and recreation of general interest to teachers, all issues contain some material which is specifically concerned with teachers' continuing professional education.

Insight

The National Conference of Teachers' Centre Leaders publishes this journal three times per year. It concentrates mainly on teachers' in-service education. Subscriptions for three issues (post free) of £3 should be sent to Hugh Thomas, Neath Teachers' Centre, Cae Rhys Ddu Road, Cimla, Neath, West Glamorgan SA11 1HZ.

Education Today

This is the journal of the College of Preceptors. Published three times a year, it is described as 'an international digest of educational literature' much of which is in-service in character. The annual subscription is £4 (post free). The publication is obtainable from the College of Preceptors, Coppice Row, Theydon Bois, Epping, Essex CM16 7DN.

Many other periodicals feature occasional articles on in-service education. These publications range from those of general educational type such as the LEA journal *Education* or the *Times Educational Supplement*, to those which are more academic such as the *British Journal of Teacher Education*. The first two of the above-mentioned appear, of course, weekly while the latter appears three times per year. It is not uncommon for some journals to devote the whole of an issue to in-service education matters, two fairly recent instances being *Trends in Education* (no. 3, autumn issue, 1977) and *Cambridge Journal of Education* (vol. 9, nos 2 and 3 combined, Michaelmas term 1979). Also, nearly all subject and special interest educational bodies publish their own 'house' journals and these, too, include articles featuring in-service matters from time to time.

B BOOKS

There are not many books written specifically on in-service education. Here is a fairly comprehensive list of books, nearly all of which are still in print.

E. ADAMS (ed.) (1975), *In-Service Education and Teachers' Centres* (Oxford: Pergamon).
This book is not, as its title would suggest, mainly concerned with teachers' centres. Written soon after the 1972 White Paper on Education, it examines many of the broad ensuing issues of in-service education.

R. BOLAM, G. SMITH and H. CANTER (1978), *LEA Advisers and the Mechanisms of Innovation* (Slough: NFER).
The authors have filled a serious gap in the literature in analysing the role of the advisory service, not least with respect to in-service provision for teachers.

B. CANE (1969), *In-Service Training* (Slough: NFER).
Though now somewhat dated, Cane's survey on teachers' professional problems and in-service needs is still worth reading.

M. COLLINS (1969), *Students into Teachers* (London: Routledge & Kegan Paul).
This was one of the first books of a series which concentrated on the problems and needs of probationary teachers.

N. EVANS (1978), *Beginning Teaching in Professional Partnership* (London: Hodder & Stoughton).
Unlike almost all books dealing with induction/probation, this starts with the final year of initial teacher education at college. The author stresses that there should be harmony between this final year and the probationary year of teaching. A theme of the book is that there is a need for more co-operation between teacher-educators and colleagues in schools.

F. J. GOODWIN (1973), *First Teaching Appointment* (Oxford: Blackwell).
A simple guide aimed at probationers about the problems, needs and opportunities likely to be faced at the start of their careers.

G. HAIGH (1972), *Beginning Teaching* (London: Pitman).
The scope of this book is similar to that of the previous one.

C. HANNAM, P. SMYTH and N. STEPHENSON (1976), *The First Year of Teaching* (Harmondsworth: Penguin).
Another book for new teachers, this is of equal value to students at college

about to undertake teaching practice and newly qualified members of the profession. It is more slanted towards the basics of teaching rather than with suggesting how difficulties may be overcome in classroom and school.

E. S. HENDERSON (1978), *The Evaluation of In-Service Teacher Training* (London: Croom Helm).
Undoubtedly, this study is rapidly becoming the definitive work on the subject of evaluation in the in-service area. It is essential reading for all teachers responsible for developing the school's SFSD programme.

D. J. JOHNSTON (1971), *Teachers' In-Service Education* (Oxford: Pergamon).
Sadly out of print, the book affords the only general review of in-service education in this country that has been written. It describes the variety of provision sometimes called the 'in-service jungle'.

R. W. MORANT (1977), *The Professional Centre: Its Potential as a Major In-Service Institution* (Crewe: Crewe and Alsager College of Higher Education).
The professional centre was proposed in the James Report of 1972 on Teacher Education and Training as a new type of educational institution for the development of teachers' in-service education. This work offers a number of suggestions on how the concept could be further understood and advanced.

N. OTTY (1972), *Learner Teacher* (Harmondsworth: Penguin).
A beginning teacher's experiences written as a diary of the postgraduate year at a university institute of education and secondary school during the probationary year, the book provides case-study material for those hoping to improve present-day procedures in teacher education.

C. REDKNAP (1977), *Focus on Teachers' Centres* (Slough: NFER).
This is not the first book on teachers' centres, but it is the first to examine the movement analytically though not particularly critically. The direct relevance of centres to in-service education and their links with schools and other educational bodies is drawn out in the book.

L. RUBIN (ed.) (1978), *The In-Service Education of Teachers* (Boston, Mass.: Allyn & Bacon).
A collection of essays on 'trends, processions and prescriptions', this book is American in origin and context. Nevertheless, it does have applicability to many of the issues being experienced in this country.

R. THORNBURY (ed.) (1973), *Teachers' Centres* (London: Darton, Longman & Todd).
This work consists of a collection of essays loosely grouped round the theme of teachers' centres. In particular, the last three chapters dealing with centres in city and country and with their future may be of greatest interest to readers in school.

J. WALTON and J. RUCK (eds) (1975), *Resources and Resources Centres* (London: Ward Lock Educational).

A major task of teachers of a school planning in-service work will be to make decisions on resources. This book provides useful background, external and internal to the school.

D. WARWICK (1975), *School-Based In-Service Education* (Edinburgh: Oliver & Boyd).
This book was the first in this country to consider how in-service education could take place at school for the benefit of the staff rather than in the traditional form at college or university.

R. WATKINS (ed.) (1973), *In-Service Training: Structure and Content* (London: Ward Lock Educational).
One of a small number of books that took up discussion of some of the issues raised in the James Report. The book includes a chapter on the role of the school in in-service work.

C PAMPHLETS AND BOOKLETS

There is a fairly large number of publications of this type. When out of print all may be borrowed from educational libraries at university institutes of education to which serving teachers normally have access.

P. E. BANKS, N. C. BURGESS and T. D. COOK (1978), *North Western Regional In-Service Enquiry*, report of working party on behalf of North West Associated Education Authorities and North Western Regional Advisory Council for Further Education.
The report, which contains some useful statistical data, was concerned with identifying and co-ordinating in-service provision in the north-west of England.

C. R. BERESFORD and C. G. DODD (1977), *In-Service Education: The Preferences of Teachers in the Cambridge Area*, survey report for the Cambridge Area INSET Committee.
A helpful LEA study backed up with statistical material.

R. BOLAM (1973), *Induction Programmes for Probationary Teachers*, an action research report, University of Bristol.
A detailed study of the needs, problems and advantages associated with the mounting of experimental induction courses.

R. BOLAM (1976), *Innovation in In-Service and Training of Teachers*, report prepared for the Centre of Educational Research and Innovation (CERI), Organisation for Economic Co-operation and Development (distributors: HMSO).
Background reading on some concepts and typologies of, and practical approaches to, in-service education.

R. BOLAM and K. BAKER (eds) (1975), *The Teacher Induction Pilot Schemes (TIPS) Project*, national conference report, University of Bristol School of Education.
A first report on the two official induction schemes in Liverpool and Northumberland and the twelve unofficial schemes.

R. BOLAM, K. BAKER and A. McMAHON (1979), *The Teacher Induction Schemes (TIPS) Project*, national evaluation report, University of Bristol School of Education.
The final report of the DES-funded national project on teacher induction in England and Wales.

R. BOLAM, K. BAKER, A. McMAHON, J. DAVIS and C. McCABE (eds) (1977), *1977 National Conference on Teacher Induction*, conference papers, University of Bristol School of Education.
The second evaluation report on the official and unofficial induction schemes.

H. BRADLEY (1974), *In-Service Education after the White Paper*, a survey for the Nottingham Area Training Organisation, University of Nottingham School of Education.
Another local survey, this time of teachers' opinions.

CLWYD EDUCATION DEPARTMENT (undated, c. 1978), *In-Service Education for Teachers*, an INSET model for the 1980s.
This short paper outlines the in-service problems and needs experienced by one LEA, proposes strategies and makes recommendations for dealing with them.

J. DAVIS (1979), *The Liverpool Induction Pilot Scheme: A Summative Report*, Liverpool University School of Education and City of Liverpool Education Department.
A final report on one of the two official induction schemes by the local external evaluator.

B. E. DAY (1976), *In-Service Education & Training*, Report of a working party, Oxfordshire County Council.
An evaluation of existing in-service provision in the county area, with appropriate recommendations. The study partly overlaps that of the Oxford ATO (see E. S. Henderson *et al.*).

J. DEAN (ed.) (1979), *Inset and the Advisory Service*, Occasional Paper No. 2, National Association of Inspectors and Educational Advisors.
A paper that will give teachers who read it a less usual insight into the requirements of educational innovation as seen by advisory colleagues.

DEPARTMENT OF EDUCATION AND SCIENCE (1970), *Survey of In-Service Training for Teachers, 1967*, Statistics of Education – Special Series No. 2 (London: HMSO).
Though it now requires to be brought up to date, this detailed study is one of the few of its kind to shed light on the in-service scene. It is still worth referring to.

DEPARTMENT OF EDUCATION AND SCIENCE (1978), 'Induction and in-service training of teachers: 1978 survey', *Statistical Bulletin*, issue 8/78.
This survey gives limited information on the volume and cost of induction and other in-service education in the maintained sector. It is based on returns from eighty-eight LEAs.

DEPARTMENT OF EDUCATION AND SCIENCE (1978), *Making Induction Work*, a paper produced by the DES at the invitation of the Induction and In-service Training Sub-Committee of the Advisory Committee on the Supply and Training of Teachers.
This modest work is described in a foreword as 'a practical guide to the induction of new teachers based on the experience of the pilot schemes in Liverpool and Northumberland and other schemes'.

DEPARTMENT OF EDUCATION AND SCIENCE (1978), *Making INSET Work*, a paper produced by the DES at the invitation of the Induction and In-service Training Sub-Committee of the Advisory Committee on the Supply and Training of Teachers.
Unlike the previous paper on induction, this discussion paper gives some valuable leads to developing a school-focused programme.

M. ERAUT (1972), *In-Service Education for Innovation*, Occasional Paper No. 4, National Council for Educational Technology.
Contains two chapters which are particularly worth reading. One is 'The training of consultants' and the other, 'The implementation of a consultancy based system of in-service education'.

GLOUCESTERSHIRE EDUCATION COMMITTEE (1975), *The In-Service Needs of Gloucestershire Teachers*, report of working party on assessment of teachers' in-service needs.
Another local survey.

G. HAMMOND (1975), *A Survey of ATO/DES Courses 1971—1974*, report of joint working party, Association of Institute and School of Education In-Service Tutors and the University Council for the Education of Teachers.
Fills one of the many gaps in our knowledge of in-service course provision.

E. S. HENDERSON, G. W. PERRY and M. M. SPENCER (1975), *The Co-ordination of In-Service Training for Teachers*, project report, Department of Educational Studies, University of Oxford.
The report examines the scale and nature of existing in-service provision in the Oxford ATO area and makes appropriate recommendations for improvement. Of special interest is the data given on school-based in-service work taking place in primary schools.

B. HILL, K. DOBSON AND C. RICHES (1976), *The Professional Tutor*, a bibliography, Hatfield Polytechnic.
This is divided for convenience into separate sections on: the professional tutor, school practice, probation, in-service education, staff development, and so on.

I. LEWIS (1975), *In-Service Training in York*, survey of teachers' views, Education Department, University of York.
Yet another local sounding of teachers' opinions.

LIVERPOOL EDUCATION COMMITTEE (1975), *A Handbook of Suggestions for Teacher Tutors*, Education Department, City of Liverpool.

This guide was designed for tutors working both for the LEA and outside it. It was based on the experience of the first year of the Liverpool pilot induction scheme for new teachers.

C. McCABE (1978), *Induction in Northumberland*, a shortened evaluation, School of Education, University of Newcastle upon Tyne.
The writer, external evaluator of the Northumberland pilot induction scheme, brings together in one brief document descriptions of how the evaluation was carried out, the scheme and its outcomes.

S. PRATT (1973), *Staff Development in Education*, the proceedings of the first annual conference of the British Educational Administration Society, Councils and Education Press.
For anyone wishing to widen their thoughts on the subject, this is essential reading.

SCHOOLS COUNCIL (1974), *Dissemination and In-Service Training*, report of working party, Schools Council Pamphlet 14.
It exposed the problems and difficulties of disseminating information on curriculum development projects and explored how in-service education might be used as a medium for this dissemination.

J. K. TAYLOR and I. R. DALE (1971), *A Survey of Teachers in their First Year of Service*, University of Bristol.
The first detailed piece of work undertaken in this country. The data obtained was influential in establishing the Liverpool, Northumberland and other LEA induction schemes which operated in the mid-1970s.

H. TURNBULL and N. FERGUSON (eds) (1974), *In-Service Training in Colleges of Education*, Aberdeen College of Education.
A booklet containing several essays on in-service provision in colleges of education in Scotland, plus the results of a survey which took place in the Manchester area of primary schoolteachers' opinions on in-service matters.

D SOME NATIONAL BODIES

Department of Education and Science
The Department annually publishes two prospectuses giving details of in-service courses in England and Wales:

Long courses for teachers. This publication provides details of courses offered by universities, polytechnics and colleges, viz.:
(*a*) courses for higher degrees, full-time and part-time;
(*b*) in-service B.Ed. degree courses, full-time and part-time;
(*c*) special courses of advanced study, full-time and part-time (mostly leading to postgraduate, advanced and professional diplomas validated by universities or the CNAA);
(*d*) one-year full-time (or equivalent part-time) courses;
(*e*) one-term full-time courses for teachers of handicapped children;
(*f*) other one-year full-time (or equivalent part-time) courses;

(*g*) other one-term full-time courses;

(*h*) part-time courses of less than the equivalent of one year's full-time duration; and

(*i*) courses of professional training in educational psychology.

The prospectus includes the names and addresses of university schools/ departments/institutes of education, and so on, as well as polytechnics and colleges offering these courses. Also, it lists a selection of recent publications on education topics available through HMSO. (The full list of DES priced publications, *Sectional List 2*, is obtainable free from any government bookshop or by sending to HMSO, PO Box 569, London SE1 9NH.)

Short courses for teachers. This second prospectus gives details of courses organised by the Department and the Welsh Office Education Department and which are held under the direction of members of HM Inspectorate. NB It should be mentioned that these DES short courses are frequently oversubscribed, so early application is essential. Also, although maintenance has to be paid for, tuition is free.

Free copies of both prospectuses are distributed about Christmas-time to all maintained establishments via LEAs from whom additional copies may sometimes be obtained. In the event of difficulty, extra copies can be obtained direct from the DES, Teachers Branch F, Elizabeth House, 39 York Road, London SE1 7PH, and the Welsh Office Education Department, Government Buildings, Ty Glas Road, Llanishen, Cardiff.

The DES issues a number of other free publications. Possibly the most important of these is the series Reports on Education. As a rule, two or three reports come out annually giving information on education policy. Recent reports relevant to in-service education include:

No. 84 *Helping New Teachers: The Induction Year*, March 1976

No. 88 *In-Service Training: The Role of Colleges and Departments*, April 1977

No. 89 *Teacher Induction: Pilot Schemes Progress*, May 1977

A list of free publications can be obtained from the DES, Room 2/11, Elizabeth House, 39 York Road, London SE1 7PH.

College of Preceptors

The College, established for well over a century by Royal Charter, defines its work as being 'mainly in the provision of courses and qualifications for the further professional education of serving teachers'. To meet this aim, it awards in-service qualifications at three levels of attainments: associate, licentiate and fellow.

Associate of the College of Preceptors (ACP).This qualification is open to any qualified teacher serving in school who has completed his period of probation satisfactorily. He may choose a scheme of study in accordance with his wishes and his eligibility from the following:

(a) *The Foundation Scheme*: Four subjects, including 'Methods of Teaching', are studied. *Trained* qualified teachers may claim exemption from the three subjects other than 'Methods of Teaching'.

(b) *Alternative Scheme A*: This is open to teachers on a Scale 2 post or above who have taught for five or more years. The work consists of writing a 5,000-word dissertation on 'Methods of Organising a School and its Curriculum'.

(c) *Alternative Scheme B*: Newly qualified teachers within two years of completing their probation may opt for this scheme which substitutes 'Resources for Learning and the Teacher in the Community' as a subject in place of 'Methods of Teaching'.

Teachers serving in FE are covered by two other schemes, Alternative Schemes C and D.

Licentiate of the College of Preceptors (LCP). Under new regulations, the licentiate can be obtained by first studying for a diploma. The full choice includes:

   Diploma in Primary Education (Dip. Prim. Ed.)
   Diploma in Secondary Education (Dip. Sec. Ed.)
   Diploma in Further Education (Dip. FE)
   Diploma in School Management Studies (Dip. SMS)
   Diploma in Special Education (Dip. Sp. Ed.)
   Diploma in Curriculum Studies
   Diploma in Multi-Cultural Studies.

After completing a diploma which stands as a terminal qualification in its own right, further study leads to the award of the licentiate, equivalent in standard to a first degree. Alternatively, the licentiate can be studied for as a complete three-part course.

Fellow of the College of Preceptors (FCP). This is the highest qualification awarded by the College and is equivalent to an MA in Education. It is gained by presentation of a thesis.

Regulations of all these qualifications, including their patterns of study, can be obtained from:

   The Secretary,
   The College of Preceptors,
   Coppice Row,
   Theydon Bois,
   Epping,
   Essex CM16 7DN.

The list is:

   ACP Foundation Scheme
   ACP Alternatives A, B, C and D (in separate booklets)

LCP Regulations & Syllabuses Part I
LCP Regulations & Syllabuses Part II
LCP Regulations & Syllabuses Part III
Diploma in School Management Studies
Diploma in Special Education
Diploma in Primary, Secondary or Further Education (in one booklet)
Diploma in Curriculum Studies
Diploma in Multi-Cultural Studies
FCP Regulations

(A charge is made for most sets of regulations.)

Council for National Academic Awards
The Council, whose importance for teachers' in-service education has increased rapidly in recent years, now validates by far the greater number of award-bearing programmes and courses in the United Kingdom. An information booklet, *The Council: Its Place in British Higher Education*, gives a brief description of the CNAA and its work. For those wishing to read a more substantial volume on the establishment and development of the Council from 1964, there is the book, *Design for Degrees*, by Michael Lane (1975), published by Macmillan (London). A regular and up-to-date picture of the Council's work can be obtained by reading its *Annual Report* which comes out in July of each year. This includes a review of the previous year, details of the membership of the Council and its principal committees, boards and panels, as well as statistical information on the qualifications that have been awarded. The report also gives the names of the Council's senior officers.

A handsheet entitled *Commentary* is published three times a year by the Council. This contains news about the people connected with the Council and institutions whose courses are CNAA-validated.

In-service qualifications which are awarded by the Council are:

In-Service B.Ed. Degree. Normally, programmes for the degree involve one year's full-time or three years' part-time study leading to the Unclassified or Honours degree. Sometimes, Honours programmes require four years' part-time study. All programmes leading to the degree are taught.

Diploma in Professional Studies in Education; Postgraduate Diploma.
Under the Council's present regulations, both qualifications require one year's full-time or two years' (sometimes three) part-time study involving attendance at taught programmes.

As its title implies, the first of these qualifications is a post-experience diploma the award of which depends on a programme the main aim of which must be to enhance professional practice in school or classroom.

The postgraduate diploma, strictly speaking, is intended as its name implies for graduate teachers. However, it is the normal procedure for entry requirements to permit enrolment of non-graduates with equivalent qualifications and/or professional experience. Diplomas of this kind emphasise the acquisition of new or advanced academic knowledge.

M.Ed. Degree. This Degree is the product of taught programmes of study usually requiring three years' part-time work. These programmes, although intellectually more demanding than those leading to professional diplomas, have the main aim of enhancing professional practice.

A programme of study is usually open to graduate and non-graduate qualified teachers. However, the latter must possess an advanced diploma in an appropriate educational discipline.

M.Phil. Degree; PhD Degree. Both these degrees can be obtained by means of individual programmes of supervised research.

In addition, there are a small number of institutions of higher education which offer taught programmes of study leading to the CNAA-validated MA in Education.

Details of all taught programmes and institutions offering them are given in publications which are issued by the Council in September annually:

Directory of First Degree and Diploma of Higher Education Courses
and
Directory of Postgraduate and Post-Experience Courses.

Both directories contain brief descriptions of all CNAA-validated programmes of study, together with the names and addresses of the colleges or polytechnics at which they can be studied.

Apart from the book by Michael Lane which may be ordered through the usual booksellers, all the above CNAA publications are obtainable, free of charge, from the Council, together with a full list of publications:

Council for National Academic Awards,
344–54 Gray's Inn Road,
London WC1X 8BP.

Correspondence Colleges
The Council for the Accreditation of Correspondence Colleges (CACC) publishes a list of colleges which have been awarded accreditation. This is obtainable free from:

The Secretary,
Council for the Accreditation of Correspondence Colleges,
27 Marylebone Road,
London NW1 5JS.

The list gives the names, addresses and telephone numbers of several colleges which provide academic and professional courses relevant to the in-service education of teachers.

Schools Council
The Council publishes a wide range of materials giving information, news and articles, and so on, about its work:

Information leaflets. Copies of individual leaflets can be obtained on request free from the Council by writing to the Information Section at:

Schools Council,
160 Great Portland Street,
London W1N 6LL.

The leaflets are on these subjects:

Schools Council: Organisation and Representation
Schools Council: Field Officers
Schools Council: Publications
Schools Council: Information Services
Schools Council: Projects
Schools Council: Learning and Teaching Schemes in Science
Schools Council: Learning and Teaching Schemes in Mathematics
Schools Council: Learning and Teaching Schemes in the Humanities and Social Sciences
Schools Council: Learning and Teaching Schemes in English
Schools Council: Learning and Teaching Schemes in Reading
Schools Council: Learning and Teaching Schemes in Environmental Education
Schools Council: Examinations
Schools Council: Evaluation
Schools Council: Learning and Teaching Schemes in the Nursery Age Range
Schools Council: Learning and Teaching Schemes in the Age Range 5–13
Schools Council: Learning and Teaching Schemes for Children with Learning Difficulties.

The three leaflets which have been asterisked are particularly useful. Commenting briefly on their contents in turn:

The field officers of the Council are always willing to visit individual schools given sufficient notice, to talk about projects and other aspects of the Council's work and policies.
The information services include the reference and study facilities located at the Schools Council headquarters in London as well as at various regional information centres throughout the country. All these centres contain collections of curriculum material which are available for viewing.
The leaflet on publications gives full detail of all books, booklets and pamphlets issued under the direction of the Council. Free material, incidentally, must be ordered direct from the Council, while much of the costed material should be ordered through booksellers.

Schools Council News is an eight-page newsletter that comes out once a term. It contains comments, news and articles on the work of the Council, as well as about its projects and publications. Although it is sent free to all schools, individuals can obtain their own copies free by contacting the Information Section at the Schools Council headquarters.

Comprehensive information on all Schools Council projects is conveyed via the *Project Profiles and Index*. This consists of a set of sheets describing every project (of which there are approximately 170). Normally, the set is published collectively under the above title every two years. However, there is constant revision of the profiles of each project, and updated sheets are issued with *Schools Council Link*, a bi-monthly bulletin which includes progress reports, dates of forthcoming conferences and details of new publications in respect of existing or new projects. The Schools Council charges an annual subscription fee (of several pounds) for *Link* plus one complete new edition of the *Project Profile and Index*. Details of this service are obtainable from the Information Section.

Like many other public bodies, the Council brings out an annual report. Published by Evans/Methuen, the *Schools Council Report*, which is priced, can be ordered through booksellers.

Of the 170 or so Schools Council projects, several are specifically concerned with aspects of in-service education. They are thus likely to be of interest to teachers planning SFSD programmes. These projects are:

> *Impact and Take-Up of Schools Council Projects*
> *Making the Most of the Short In-Service Course on Curriculum Development*
> *Teachers' Centres: Their Role and Functioning.*

Details of these projects and others, many of which include objectives concerning in-service education and dissemination, are to be found in the appropriate project profiles.

The Open University

Offering a wide variety of study opportunities for serving teachers amongst adults generally, the Open University provides three distinctive programmes of study:

Bachelor of Arts degree (BA). This is a general degree which can be taken without or with honours. Anyone over the age of 21 living in the United Kingdom is eligible to be a student on the programme since no academic entry qualifications are required. Admission each year depends on a 'first-come first-served' policy. Applications for admission should normally be made in the period January to May for the following year.

The programme of study consists of arts courses or science courses or a combination of both. These courses are constructed out of correspondence and broadcast materials which are reinforced by tutorial and counselling services.

To obtain the ordinary degree requires successfully studying courses (each valued at half or a whole credit) which altogether tally up to a total of six credits. To obtain the Honours degree requires studying courses which together bring eight credits.

Qualified teachers should normally be eligible, by virtue of previous full-time study (or the part-time equivalent) for a maximum of three credit exemptions, thereby reducing the total minimum number of credits required by study on the programme to three for the ordinary and five for the honours degree.

The *Guide for Applicants* for BA degree courses is obtainable with an application form, free, from:

The Admissions Office,
The Open University,
PO Box 48,
Milton Keynes MK7 6AB.

Correspondence in connection with matters to do with credit exemptions should be directed to:

Advanced Standing Office,
The Open University,
PO Box 80,
Milton Keynes MK7 6AS.

Associate Student Programme. The university offers several types of course under this heading, namely:

(a) Many of the courses included in the programme of undergraduate study leading to the BA degree can be taken on a 'one-off' basis. Students completing such courses and having passed a voluntary examination are awarded a course certificate.

(b) There is a growing number of advanced courses prepared by the university's Post-Experience Courses Unit which have vocational and therefore in-service educational relevance. For instance, four separate but related courses on offer lead jointly to the award of the diploma in reading development.

(c) Another group of courses are offered by the university in association with various outside bodies. These are the community education courses which last for eight to ten weeks and are not designed to be studied at university level.

Applications for entry to courses in the associate student programme normally are made in the period from May to October of the previous year. Full details are provided in the *Associate Student Prospectus* which can be obtained free from:

The Associate Student Central Office,
The Open University,
PO Box 76,
Milton Keynes MK7 6AN.

Higher Degrees. The Open University offers the following degrees at this level:

> Bachelor of Philosophy (B.Phil.)
> Master of Philosophy (M.Phil.)
> Doctor of Philosophy (PhD)
> Doctor of Letters (D.Litt.)
> Doctor of Science (D.Sc.)

At present, these qualifications can only be obtained as a result of undertaking a research programme (or in the case of the B. Phil. only, by making a critical review of a given field). But the university hopes to make higher degrees through coursework and examination available in the near future.

Normally, higher degrees of the Open University can be worked for only by candidates with an upper second class honours first degree or above.

Full details of all higher degrees are given in the booklet *Postgraduate Prospectus and Student Handbook* for the current year. This can be obtained free from:

> The Higher Degree Office,
> The Open University,
> PO Box 49,
> Milton Keynes MK7 6AD.

Two other OU addresses may also be useful to readers. These are:

> Open University Educational Enterprises Ltd,
> 12 Cofferidge Close,
> Stony Stratford,
> Milton Keynes MK11 1BY

(for purchase of books, films and other course materials)

> The Student Enquiry Service,
> The Open University,
> PO Box 71,
> Milton Keynes MK7 6AG

(for details of times and dates of radio and TV programmes)

Some Other Useful Addresses

> BBC PUBLICATIONS,
> 35 Marylebone High Street,
> London W1A 1AA

DEPARTMENT OF EDUCATION FOR NORTHERN IRELAND,
Rathgael House,
Balloo Road,
Bangor,
Co. Down BT19 2PR

INDEPENDENT BROADCASTING AUTHORITY,
70 Brompton Road,
Knightsbridge,
London SW3

NATIONAL INSTITUTE OF ADULT EDUCATION,
19b De Montfort Street,
Leicester LE1 7GE

SCOTTISH EDUCATION DEPARTMENT,
New St Andrew's House,
St James Centre,
Edinburgh EH1 3TD

SCOTTISH INSTITUTE OF ADULT EDUCATION,
96 Woodside Terrace Lane,
Glasgow G3

WELSH EDUCATION OFFICE,
Government Buildings, Phase 2,
Ty Glas Road,
Llanishen,
Cardiff

WORKERS EDUCATIONAL ASSOCIATION,
Temple House,
9 Upper Berkeley Street,
London W1

Index

advanced further education pool 23
advisers 96,103
Advisory Committee on the Supply and Training of Teachers 4
Ashmead School, Reading 31–2, 38, 41, 65, 77
award-bearing courses 19–20

B.Ed. degree 25
Benfield Comprehensive School, Newcastle upon Tyne 30, 43
Bolam, Ray 102
Bristol Polytechnic 102
British Broadcasting Corporation 18
Burnham Committee 104

Cambridge Institute of Education 34
Cane, Brian 2
caravan trailers 98
centre–periphery diffusion 14
Chesterton School, Cambridge 34–5, 38, 96–7
City and Guilds Institute 22
college lecturers 96
College of Preceptors 17–18, 22
colleges of higher education 17–18, 98
command meeting 71–3
committee meeting 71
conditions of service 104
consultancy, internal and external 102
consultative or advisory committees 27
Council for National Academic Awards 16, 18, 21–2
curriculum development 54–5

Davies, Sefton 102
Department of Education and Science 15, 20, 96
  handbook of long courses 19
  regional courses 15

educational interest associations 17
Ellis, Anita 33
empirical/rational policies 76
evaluation techniques 90–4
expenses for teachers 99–100
external degrees 22

Fell, Ronald 32
formative evaluation 85–94
formulation of policies 67–8

Gittings Committee 26
Green Paper on Education 25–6

Hartcliffe School, Bristol 33–4, 38, 41, 43, 97
Heathland School, Hounslow 35–6, 98
Henderson, Euan 3, 26–7
Her Majesty's Inspectors 96
HMI survey on primary curriculum 5–6
Homerton College 34, 96

Independent Broadcasting Authority 18
innovation 52
in-service committee 77
in-service objectives 3–4
in-service training 1–4, 77
INSET 3
institutes of higher education 16–17
institutional recognition or accreditation 22
inventory of equipment and materials 97–8

James Committee 2, 15
Joint Board of Library Association and School Library Association 21
judgement in education 81–2

leadership of programme 45

limitations of school-based
in-service education 41
Lincoln, Abraham 82
local education authorities 15–16,
23, 98–100, 102–3
London University 22

Martin, Robert 30
Mathematical Association 17, 21
measurement in education 80
members of health and social
services 96
Moons Moat Nursery and First
School 36–8, 43
motivation of teachers 9–10

National Association for Gifted
Children 17
National Association for Remedial
Education 17
National Association for the
Teaching of English 17
National Association of
Schoolmasters/Union of
Women Teachers 18
National Marriage Guidance
Council 33, 97
National Union of Teachers 17–18
Newsom Committee 26
normative/re-educative strategies
76–7
Norton Priory Comprehensive
School, Runcorn 30–1, 38, 43,
97
Nursery School Association of
Great Britain and Northern
Ireland 17

occasional holidays 104
Open University 16
organisation development 54–5

parents 96
Pepper, Ron 29
Perry, Pauline 42
Plowden Committee 26
polytechnics 16, 98
Poster, Cyril 52

postgraduate certificate in
education 25
power/coercive strategies 76
Privy Council 21
probation 7
process consultancy 101
professional development 1–2

qualitative evidence 81–2
quantitative evidence 81–2
quinquennial grant 23

rates 23
redeployment, external and
internal 10
renovation 52
representative council 70
Rivington and Blackrod High
School, Bolton 32–3, 37–8,
41, 45, 49

salaries of teachers 23
Samuel, Geoffrey 35
school governors 96
Schools Council 17–18
field officers 96
Schools Regulations 104
secondment of teachers 20
self-validation 21
Shipman, Marten 80
Simmons, Lillian 36
Skilbeck, Malcolm 55
staff development 38
staff open meeting 70–3
Stenhouse, Lawrence 31
subject interest associations 17
summative evaluation 84–5, 89–90
supplementary courses 26

targets of evaluation 84
task consultancy 101–2
teachers' centres 15–17
teachers' centre wardens 96, 103
teachers' certificate 25
teachers' unions 17–18
Thomas Calton School, Peckham
29–30, 38, 98
travelling libraries 98

Truman, Harry S. 83
tuition fees 23

universities 16, 22, 98
University Grants Committee 23
university lecturers 96

validation, external 20–2
validation, internal 21

Warwick, David 31, 41
White Paper on Education 15
Wood, Hugh 34